Skopje in Three D

Welcome to Skopje, a city of contrasts and a melting pot of cultures. Nestled in the heart of the Balkans, Skopje beckons travelers with its rich history, vibrant atmosphere, and warm hospitality. This travel guide is your passport to unlocking the secrets of this captivating capital of North Macedonia.

Skopje, with its roots tracing back to ancient times, has witnessed the rise and fall of empires, the passage of conquerors, and the blending of diverse civilizations.

Today, it stands as a testament to the resilience and spirit of its people. As you traverse its streets, you'll encounter a fusion of architectural styles, where Byzantine domes, Ottoman minarets, and modernist structures coexist harmoniously.

Prepare to be enchanted as you stroll along the cobblestone lanes of the Old Bazaar, one of the oldest marketplaces in the Balkans. Lose yourself amidst the maze of shops, savoring the aroma of freshly brewed coffee and the sweet scent of Turkish delight. Engage with local artisans, as they skillfully craft traditional crafts and share stories of generations past.

Skopje's city center is a canvas of grandeur, showcasing the ambitious Skopje 2014 project. This transformative endeavor has reimagined the cityscape, adorning it with grand statues, fountains, and majestic buildings that pay homage to Macedonia's historical figures and cultural heritage. As you explore these magnificent landmarks, be prepared to be awestruck by the scale and ambition of this artistic vision.

Beyond its architectural wonders, Skopje offers a treasure trove of cultural experiences. Discover the poignant stories housed within the museums and galleries, where art and history intertwine. Immerse yourself in the lively festivals and celebrations that breathe life into the city, providing glimpses into its vibrant traditions and customs.

But Skopje is not only a city of stone and history; it is also a gateway to natural wonders. Just a short distance away, the breathtaking Matka Canyon beckons nature enthusiasts and adventure seekers alike. Lose yourself in its emerald waters, surrounded by towering cliffs and lush greenery, and explore the hidden caves that hold secrets of the past.

As you embark on this journey through Skopje, let your senses be your guide. Taste the flavors of Macedonian cuisine, from hearty grilled meats to delectable pastries. Listen to the sounds of street musicians and traditional folk music, filling the air with a melodic rhythm. Engage with the locals, who embody the spirit of Skopje and are eager to share their love for their city.

This travel guide is designed to help you navigate the wonders of Skopje, to unearth its hidden gems, and to create memories that will last a lifetime. So, pack your bags, open your heart to new experiences, and let Skopje weave its magic around you.

Welcome to Skopje, where history, culture, and natural beauty converge in a tapestry of enchantment. Let the journey begin!

Contents

1. Introduction

Nestled in the heart of North Macedonia, the city of Skopje beckons travelers with its rich history, architectural marvels, and vibrant cultural tapestry. Situated along the banks of the Vardar River, Skopje has served as a crossroads of civilizations for centuries, resulting in a cityscape that is as diverse as it is captivating.

One of the most enchanting aspects of Skopje is its deep-rooted history. As you wander through its streets, you can't help but feel the echoes of ancient civilizations that have left their indelible mark. Roman ruins whisper tales of the city's past glory, while Byzantine churches stand as stoic reminders of its spiritual heritage. The streets themselves seem to breathe with the weight of Ottoman influence, as traditional architecture merges seamlessly with contemporary designs.

A testament to Skopje's architectural prowess is the Skopje 2014 project. This ambitious undertaking sought to transform the city's appearance by erecting neoclassical and monumental buildings. As you stroll through Skopje's streets, you'll be greeted by an eclectic blend of architectural styles, creating a visual spectacle that is truly unique. From the grandeur of the Macedonian Parliament to the striking statues that adorn the city's squares, Skopje offers a feast for the eyes at every turn.

Yet, Skopje's allure extends far beyond its physical beauty. The city's cultural diversity is one of its greatest strengths. Skopje is a melting pot of various ethnic communities, each contributing their unique traditions, languages, and cuisines. Immerse yourself in the rich Macedonian culture as you explore the bustling bazaars, where the scents of spices and the vibrant colors of traditional textiles fill the air. Engage with the remnants of Ottoman heritage, from the enchanting Turkish baths to the intricately designed mosques that dot the cityscape.

Skopje also boasts an array of landmarks and monuments that bear witness to its storied past. The iconic Stone Bridge, with its sturdy arches, stands as a symbol of the city's resilience and connection between its two halves. Venture up the winding paths to the Kale Fortress, an ancient stronghold that offers panoramic views of the city below. Discover the poignant Memorial House of Mother Teresa, honoring the Nobel laureate's humanitarian legacy.

Beyond its historical and architectural marvels, Skopje is a city that thrives on its vibrant cultural scene. Art galleries and museums showcase the works of local talents, while theaters and performance venues offer a platform for creativity to flourish. The city comes alive at night, with a buzzing nightlife that caters to all tastes, from lively bars and clubs to intimate music venues.

For nature enthusiasts, Skopje offers respite with its proximity to natural wonders. Venture beyond the city's borders to explore the breathtaking landscapes of Matka Canyon or escape to the tranquil shores of Lake Ohrid, a UNESCO World Heritage Site.

Skopje is an underrated gem of a city that tantalizes the senses with a captivating blend of history, architecture, and culture. Whether you find yourself enchanted by its historical landmarks, mesmerized by its architectural marvels, or immersed in its vibrant cultural tapestry, Skopje promises a truly unforgettable experience. It is a city where the past and present converge, leaving visitors with a profound appreciation for the rich tapestry of human history and the enduring spirit of a captivating destination.

1.1 The History of Skopje

Skopje, the capital city of North Macedonia, has a rich and diverse history that spans millennia. From its ancient origins as a strategic settlement along trade routes, through Byzantine rule and the influence of the Ottoman Empire, to its modern-day status as a vibrant cultural hub, Skopje's history is a captivating tapestry of civilizations and influences. The city's ancient period saw the rise of Roman architecture and infrastructure, while the Byzantine era left a lasting legacy of Byzantine art and religious structures. Under Ottoman rule, Skopje flourished as a center of commerce and Islamic culture, with mosques and hammams dotting the cityscape. The modern period witnessed the city's transformation into a cosmopolitan capital, with architectural developments and reconstruction projects. Exploring Skopje means embarking on a journey through time, unraveling the layers of history that have shaped this fascinating city.

The ancient period of Skopje's history, spanning from approximately 4000 BCE to 500 CE, reveals the city's emergence as a significant settlement along the crossroads of ancient civilizations. During this time, Skopje witnessed the rise and fall of various cultures, leaving behind a rich archaeological legacy.

In its early years, Skopje was inhabited by the Dardanians, an ancient Indo-European tribe. Traces of their presence can be found in the archaeological remains discovered in and around the city. As trade routes began to develop, Skopje grew in importance as a hub for commercial and cultural exchange.

One of the most influential periods in Skopje's ancient history was the Roman era. In 168 BCE, the Romans conquered the region, bringing about a period of prosperity and architectural development. Skopje, known as Scupi in Roman times, became a bustling city with well-preserved urban planning and notable infrastructure.

Under Roman rule, Skopje flourished as a center of trade and commerce, strategically located along the Via Egnatia, an important Roman road connecting the Adriatic Sea to Byzantium (present-day Istanbul). The city's development included the construction of impressive buildings such as theaters, baths, and aqueducts, showcasing the grandeur of Roman architecture.

Skopje's status as a Roman settlement continued for several centuries until the decline of the Roman Empire. With the arrival of the Goths and other migratory tribes in the 4th and 5th centuries CE, the city underwent a period of instability and transformation.

Although much of Skopje's ancient history is buried beneath the modern city, archaeological excavations have unearthed fascinating artifacts and remnants of ancient structures. Visitors can explore the Skopje Archaeological Museum to see the treasures of the ancient period, including statues, jewelry, pottery, and architectural fragments.

With the end of the Western Roman Empire, Skopje entered its Byzantine period of history from 500 to 1392. It was a time of significant cultural and religious influence that left an indelible mark on the city. As Skopje came under Byzantine control, it flourished as an important center of administration, culture, and spirituality within the Byzantine Empire.

During this period, Skopje experienced a period of architectural and artistic development influenced by Byzantine traditions. The city became adorned with magnificent churches and monasteries, displaying intricate mosaics, frescoes, and religious iconography. One of the most notable examples is the Church of St. Panteleimon, an impressive 12th-century Byzantine structure that has survived to this day.

Skopje's significance in the Byzantine Empire extended beyond its architectural contributions. The city became an important cultural center, attracting scholars, theologians, and artists who contributed to the intellectual and artistic vibrancy of the era. Byzantine writers and thinkers produced influential works in Skopje, leaving behind a rich literary heritage.

Throughout the **Byzantine period,** Skopje experienced shifting political dynamics as it changed hands between various ruling powers, including Byzantine, Bulgarian, and Serbian authorities. These transitions had an impact on the city's cultural and religious landscape, as each ruling entity left its own imprint on Skopje's architecture and traditions.

Despite political changes and occasional conflicts, Skopje remained a hub of Byzantine spirituality. Monastic communities flourished, with numerous monasteries dotting the surrounding landscapes. These spiritual centers played a vital role in preserving and disseminating Byzantine religious and cultural traditions.

Today, remnants of Skopje's Byzantine past can be discovered through archaeological excavations and visits to ancient churches. The Skopje Fortress, known as Kale, which dates back to the Byzantine period, still stands as a testament to the city's strategic importance and architectural legacy.

The Byzantine period of Skopje's history offers a glimpse into a time of artistic flourishing, spiritual devotion, and cultural exchanges within the Byzantine Empire.

Exploring the Byzantine heritage of Skopje allows visitors to appreciate the city's intricate mosaics, experience the tranquility of its ancient churches, and gain insight into the spiritual and intellectual legacy that continues to shape the city's identity.

The Ottoman period of Skopje's history, spanning from 1392 to 1912, left an indelible mark on the city, shaping its architecture, culture, and identity. As Skopje came under Ottoman rule, it transformed into a vibrant center of commerce, Islamic culture, and artistic expression.

Under **Ottoman influence**, Skopje experienced a period of urban development and expansion. The cityscape transformed with the construction of mosques, hammams (Turkish baths), and other architectural elements that showcased the distinctive Ottoman architectural style. Notable examples include the Mustafa Pasha Mosque and the Sultan Murad Mosque, both of which continue to stand as iconic symbols of Skopje's Ottoman past.

Skopje became a bustling center of trade and craftsmanship, attracting artisans, merchants, and traders from diverse backgrounds. The bazaars and markets bustled with activity, offering a vibrant display of goods and commodities from around the region. Skopje's strategic location along the trade routes of the Ottoman Empire further enhanced its economic importance.

Islamic influence permeated every aspect of Skopje's culture during the Ottoman period. The city's population grew more diverse, with communities of various ethnic and religious backgrounds coexisting within its borders. Skopje became a hub of Islamic learning, with numerous madrasas (religious schools) established to promote education and religious teachings.

The Ottoman period also left its mark on Skopje's cuisine. Traditional Ottoman dishes and flavors became integrated into the local culinary scene, adding depth and richness to the gastronomic heritage of the city. Delicacies such as *kebabs, börek* (pastry filled with meat or cheese), and *baklava* became popular, showcasing the fusion of Ottoman and local culinary traditions.

Skopje's Ottoman period came to an end with the decline of the Ottoman Empire, at which time Skopje became part of multiple states on the way to the emergence of an independent Macedonia. The modern period of Skopje's history began in 1912 and continues to the present day, representing a time of transformation, growth, and cultural renaissance. This era encompasses Skopje's evolution as a cosmopolitan capital, experiencing significant changes in urbanization, industrialization, and architectural development.

Following the **Balkan Wars in 1912**, Skopje was liberated from Ottoman rule and became part of various political entities, including **Yugoslavia.** This marked a new chapter for the city, as it underwent rapid modernization and urban development. Skopje's population grew, and the city expanded with new neighborhoods and infrastructure to accommodate its increasing size.

The **devastating earthquake of 1963** was a defining moment in Skopje's modern history. The earthquake resulted in widespread destruction, leading to a large-scale reconstruction effort. The rebuilding process became an opportunity for architects and urban planners to reimagine Skopje's cityscape. The Skopje 2014 project, initiated in the 2010s, aimed to transform the city center with new buildings and monuments, blending contemporary and neoclassical architectural styles.

Skopje's modern period witnessed significant industrial growth and economic development. The city became an industrial hub, with factories and manufacturing plants contributing to the region's economic prosperity. This period also witnessed advancements in education, healthcare, and transportation infrastructure, further enhancing the quality of life in Skopje.

Culturally, Skopje experienced a renaissance during the modern period. The city became a vibrant center of art, music, and theater. The Skopje Jazz Festival, held annually since 1981, showcases the city's love for music and attracts international artists. The Macedonian Opera and Ballet, National Theater, and numerous art galleries contribute to Skopje's thriving cultural scene.

Skopje's modern period also encompasses its journey towards independence and the establishment of the independent state of North Macedonia in 1991. This significant milestone marked a new era of self-governance and national identity for the city and its people.

Today, Skopje stands as a testament to its modern period, with a diverse architectural landscape that blends historical and contemporary elements. The city's vibrant cultural scene, bustling markets, and lively atmosphere make it an attractive destination for visitors seeking a blend of history, modernity, and cultural exploration.

Exploring Skopje's modern period means immersing oneself in its architectural wonders, experiencing its cultural events, and witnessing the spirit of resilience and progress that defines the city. Skopje's modern era represents its ongoing journey of growth, adaptation, and embracing the challenges and opportunities of the present day.

1.2 Skopje's Geography and Climate

Its geographical position is characterized by diverse landscapes, surrounded by mountains, rivers, and fertile plains.

The city is situated on the banks of the Vardar River, which flows through the heart of Skopje. The river serves as a natural centerpiece, dividing the city into two distinct parts: the old part, on the right bank, and the new part, on the left bank. Numerous bridges, including the iconic Stone Bridge, connect the two sides, creating a harmonious blend of history and modernity.

Skopje is surrounded by picturesque mountain ranges. To the north, the Vodno Mountain stands majestically, offering stunning views of the city from its peak. Mount Vodno is also home to the Millennium Cross, an iconic landmark visible from various parts of Skopje. To the east, the Skopska Crna Gora mountain range stretches, providing a scenic backdrop to the cityscape.

The climate of Skopje is characterized as transitional Mediterranean, influenced by its inland location and the surrounding mountains. Summers are typically hot and dry, with average temperatures ranging from 25 to 30 degrees Celsius (77 to 86 degrees Fahrenheit). Winters are moderately cold, with temperatures averaging around 0 degrees Celsius (32 degrees Fahrenheit). Skopje experiences all four seasons, with pleasant springs and colorful autumns.

The city receives a moderate amount of rainfall throughout the year, with the wettest months typically being April, May, and November. Snowfall is common in winter, transforming the city into a winter wonderland and offering opportunities for winter sports enthusiasts.

Skopje's geographical location in the heart of the Balkans makes it a gateway to explore the natural beauty of North

Macedonia. Within a short distance from the city, visitors can access national parks, such as Mavrovo and Pelister, which offer opportunities for hiking, skiing, and enjoying pristine nature.

The geography of Skopje, with its river, mountains, and fertile plains, contributes to the city's charm and provides a diverse range of recreational activities. Whether strolling along the riverbanks, hiking in the nearby mountains, or simply admiring the panoramic views, Skopje's geography offers something for everyone.

In conclusion, Skopje's geography is defined by its central location within North Macedonia, the presence of the Vardar River, and the surrounding mountain ranges. The city's transitional Mediterranean climate ensures a pleasant balance of seasons, with hot summers and moderately cold winters. The geographical diversity of Skopje invites visitors to explore its natural beauty, engage in outdoor activities, and appreciate the stunning landscapes that surround this vibrant capital city.

1.3 Macedonia's Economy

Macedonia, officially known as the Republic of North Macedonia ever since the 2018 Prespa Agreement, is a country that's undergone a great economic transformation in recent decades. The country transitioned from a centrally-planned economy to a market-oriented economy after 1991, and it also had to navigate a refugee crisis instigated by the Kosovo War. While the country has made great strides, there are still challenges to overcome and progress to be made.

Macroeconomic Indicators:

To understand the overall economic landscape of Macedonia, it is crucial to examine some key macroeconomic indicators. In recent years, Macedonia has experienced a stable economic growth rate, with a focus on attracting foreign direct investment (FDI) and fostering business-friendly policies. In 2021, the country's GDP stood at $12.9 billion, with a growth rate of 3.6% (World Bank, 2021). The inflation rate has remained relatively low, averaging around 1.5% in recent years, contributing to price stability and investor confidence. Additionally, the government has successfully reduced the fiscal deficit and maintained a moderate public debt-to-GDP ratio.

Key Economic Sectors:

Manufacturing and Export-Oriented Industries:
Macedonia has made significant strides in developing its manufacturing sector, which contributes significantly to its economy. The country has attracted foreign investors in automotive, textile, and electronics industries, leveraging its competitive advantage of low labor costs. Skopje, the capital city, is home to several multinational manufacturing companies, driving exports and creating employment opportunities.

Tourism: Macedonia possesses a rich cultural and natural heritage, attracting tourists from around the world. The country offers diverse attractions, including historical sites, picturesque landscapes, and outdoor activities. Skopje, Ohrid, and Bitola are among the most visited cities. The government has invested in tourism infrastructure and marketing campaigns to promote the sector's growth, contributing to job creation and foreign exchange earnings.

Information Technology and Outsourcing: Macedonia has emerged as an attractive destination for information technology (IT) and business process outsourcing (BPO) services. Skilled workforce, competitive labor costs, and favorable government policies have encouraged the growth of IT companies and startups. Skopje, in particular, has become a hub for software development, digital marketing, and customer support services, driving innovation and creating high-quality jobs.

Challenges and Reforms:

Despite its progress, Macedonia faces several challenges that need to be addressed to ensure sustained economic growth:

Unemployment and Brain Drain: High unemployment rates, especially among the youth, pose a significant challenge. Many skilled professionals opt to seek better employment opportunities abroad, leading to a brain drain and hindered economic development. The government has implemented reforms to enhance vocational training programs and promote entrepreneurship, aiming to reduce unemployment and retain talent.

Corruption and Rule of Law: Corruption remains a significant concern in Macedonia. Strengthening the rule of law, enhancing transparency, and combating corruption are crucial for creating a favorable business environment and attracting foreign investment. The government has undertaken reforms to improve the efficiency of the judiciary and enhance anti-corruption measures, demonstrating a commitment to address these issues.

Infrastructure Development: Investments in infrastructure are necessary to support economic growth and attract further investment. Upgrading transportation networks, improving energy infrastructure, and expanding broadband connectivity are vital for enhancing the country's competitiveness. Macedonia has prioritized infrastructure development, including road construction projects and the modernization of energy systems, to address these challenges.

1.4 Macedonian Language and Culture

The Macedonian language and culture hold a rich and distinct heritage that reflects the historical, linguistic, and ethnic diversity of the region. The Macedonian language belongs to the South Slavic branch of the Slavic language family and is the official language of the Republic of North Macedonia. It shares similarities with other Slavic languages, particularly Bulgarian, Serbian, and Croatian. However, it has its unique characteristics, vocabulary, and grammar that set it apart.

The Macedonian alphabet is based on the Cyrillic script, comprising 31 letters. The language has a rich literary tradition dating back centuries, with notable contributions from renowned poets, novelists, and playwrights.

Macedonian culture is a blend of various influences from its ancient past, Byzantine heritage, Ottoman rule, and more recent developments. It encompasses a diverse range of traditions, customs, arts, music, dance, and cuisine. Folklore is an essential part of the cultural fabric, preserving age-old customs, rituals, and folk dances. Traditional costumes, such as the "opanci" footwear and intricate embroidery reflect Macedonia's regional diversity and artistic craftsmanship.

Musician playing the Zurla instrument.

National music is characterized by soulful melodies, rhythms, and instruments like the **zurla, tambura, and gaida.** Traditional dances, such as the oro, are performed in intricate formations, accompanied by vibrant costumes and live music. Macedonian also has a rich literary tradition, dating back to medieval times with notable works like "The Ohrid Literary School."

A painting by Nikola Martinoski

Prominent writers and poets, such as **Koco Racin, Blaze Koneski, and Slavko Janevski,** have made significant contributions to the Macedonian literary canon. Visual arts, including painting and sculpture, also thrive in the country, with artists like **Nikola Martinoski** and **Dimitar Kondovski** gaining international recognition.

Macedonian cuisine is diverse, influenced by the country's geographic location and historical influences. Traditional dishes like **Tavče Gravče** (baked beans), **Ajvar** (roasted pepper spread), and **Pastrmajlija** (flatbread with seasoned meat) showcase the flavors and culinary traditions of the region.

Pastrmajlija

These foods are often featured at Macedonia's range of cultural and religious festivals throughout the year. The Ohrid Summer Festival is a prominent cultural event, featuring music, theater, and dance performances. Other celebrations, such as the Macedonian Independence Day and Orthodox Easter, are marked with traditional rituals and festivities.

1.5 Macedonia's Multicultural Society

Macedonians are the largest ethnic group in Macedonia, and their culture forms the foundation of the nation's identity. The Macedonian language, which belongs to the South Slavic language family, is the official language of the country. Macedonian culture encompasses a rich artistic heritage, including traditional music, dance, and folk customs.

The national costume, known as the **"opanka,"** features intricately embroidered patterns and is often worn during cultural festivals and special occasions. Macedonians celebrate traditional holidays such as **"Ilinden,"** commemorating the 1903 Ilinden Uprising, and **"Tapan,"** a celebration of the New Year. Macedonian literature, with notable figures like Kosta Racin and Blaze Koneski, has made significant contributions to the country's cultural legacy.

Albanians form the largest minority group in Macedonia, primarily residing in the western part of the country. The Albanian language, an Indo-European language with its own distinct dialects, is widely spoken within the community. Albanian culture is characterized by a rich oral tradition, expressed through music, poetry, and storytelling.

Traditional Albanian music, including the hauntingly beautiful **"Iso-Polyphony,"** is recognized as a UNESCO Intangible Cultural Heritage of Humanity. Albanians celebrate cultural events such as weddings and festivals like **"Dita e Verës"** (Summer Day), which marks the arrival of spring. Traditional Albanian cuisine, known for its delicious flavors and unique dishes, is widely appreciated throughout the country.

The **Turkish community** in Macedonia traces its roots back to the Ottoman Empire's rule. The Turkish language, belonging to the Turkic language family, is spoken within the community. Turkish cultural influences are evident in the architectural style of mosques, hammams (Turkish baths), and the bazaar areas of cities like Skopje and Bitola.

Traditional Turkish cuisine, with dishes such **as kebabs, baklava, and Turkish tea**, has become an integral part of Macedonian gastronomy. **Cig kofte**, a meat-like dish made of beans has a spicy, tangy flavor and it's well-advised to stop by the Old Bazaar and enjoy a platter of it. While kebab and other Turkish foods have become widespread throughout Europe, Skopje is one of the only cities outside of Turkey where it's easy to find. The Turkish community celebrates important religious holidays such as **"Kurban Bayram"** (Eid al-Adha) and **"Ramazan Bayram"** (Eid al-Fitr) with prayers, family gatherings, and festive meals.

Cig Kofte

The **Roma community**, also known as **Romani,** is a distinct ethnic group with a rich cultural heritage. The Roma people have their own language, Romani, which belongs to the Indo-Aryan language family. Romani music is renowned for its lively rhythms, passionate vocals, and expressive dance forms. Artists like **Esma Redžepova and Usnija Redžepova** have gained international recognition for their contributions to Romani music.

Roma crafts, such as intricate metalwork, basket weaving, and traditional dressmaking, showcase the community's artistic skills. Despite facing challenges of discrimination and socioeconomic inequality, the Roma community's vibrant cultural expressions continue to enrich the multicultural fabric of Macedonia.

Macedonia's multiculturalism is not without strife or difficulty, however. While most problems have been solved through dialogue, insurgents from Kosovo entered Macedonia and clashed with police and the army in 2001. However, there have been few acts of ethnic violence since then. Nonetheless, deep political divides exist along ethnic lines when it comes to issues like Macedonia's name dispute or joining the EU and NATO. Steady progress has been made on this issue, though, and in all likelihood Macedonia will have a vibrant multicultural future.

1.6 Famous Macedonian Musicians

Macedonia has a rich cultural heritage that comes with a deep appreciation for music, and it's produced a plethora of talented musicians who have made their mark on the region. A few Macedonian artists have broken out into global fame, but many others continue to operate within domestic and Balkan-wide music scene.

From classical composers to folk musicians and contemporary pop stars, Macedonian artists have captivated audiences with their exceptional skills and unique musical expressions. In this article, we will explore the contributions of some of the most renowned musicians from Macedonia.

Tose Proeski (1981-2007):

One of the most beloved and iconic figures in Macedonian music, Tose Proeski was a versatile singer and songwriter who achieved tremendous success in his tragically short career. Known for his powerful vocals and emotional performances, Proeski's music spanned various genres, including pop, rock, and folk. His album releases, such as "Igri Bez Granici" (Games Without Borders) and "Ako Me Poglednes Vo Oci" (If You Look Into My Eyes), became instant hits in Macedonia and throughout the Balkans. With his captivating stage presence and humanitarian efforts, Proeski left an enduring legacy in Macedonian music.

Kiril Dzajkovski:

A pioneer of electronic and fusion music, Kiril Dzajkovski has made significant contributions to the global music scene. With a career spanning over three decades, Dzajkovski seamlessly blends traditional Macedonian melodies with contemporary beats, creating a unique sonic experience. His compositions have been featured in numerous films and TV shows, gaining international recognition. Dzajkovski's groundbreaking work has not only brought Macedonian music to new audiences but has also served as an inspiration for aspiring musicians worldwide.

Aleksandar Sarievski (1922-1984):

Regarded as the "Father of Macedonian Popular Music," Aleksandar Sarievski left an indelible mark on the country's music landscape. As a composer and performer, he was known for his soulful interpretations of Macedonian folk songs. Sarievski's music resonated deeply with audiences, evoking a sense of nostalgia and national pride. His iconic songs, such as "Makedonsko Devojče" (Macedonian Girl) and "Oj, Devojče, Devojče" (Oh, Girl, Girl), continue to be cherished by generations of Macedonians, ensuring his enduring legacy in the cultural fabric of the nation.

Esma Redžepova (1943-2016):
Recognized as the "Queen of Romani Music," Esma Redžepova was a remarkable singer and humanitarian. With her powerful and captivating voice, she brought Romani music to the forefront, promoting the cultural heritage of the Roma community. Redžepova's career spanned several decades, during which she recorded numerous albums, collaborated with international artists, and represented Macedonia in the Eurovision Song Contest. Her unwavering commitment to social causes, including advocating for the rights of the Roma people, earned her widespread admiration and respect both in Macedonia and abroad.

Simon Trpčeski:
Renowned as one of the finest pianists of his generation, Simon Trpčeski has mesmerized audiences worldwide with his virtuosity and musicality. Born in the Macedonian capital of Skopje, Trpčeski has performed with prestigious orchestras and renowned conductors across the globe. His interpretations of classical masterpieces, including the works of Rachmaninoff, Prokofiev, and Mozart, have earned critical acclaim and numerous awards.

1.7 Ten Must-Know Macedonian Personalities From History

Mother Teresa

Mother Teresa (1910-1997) - Born in Skopje, Mother Teresa, originally named Anjezë Gonxhe Bojaxhiu, dedicated her life to serving the poor and disadvantaged around the world. She founded the Missionaries of Charity, an international religious congregation that provides care and support to the destitute and marginalized.

Mother Teresa's selfless work earned her worldwide recognition, and she was awarded the Nobel Peace Prize in 1979. Her compassionate and tireless efforts continue to inspire people globally, making her one of the most revered humanitarians in history. As an ethnic Albanian originally from Skopje, Mother Teresa is often honored by both Macedonians and Albanians.

Koco Racin (1908-1943) - Koco Racin was a prominent poet and key figure in Macedonian literature. His works played a vital role in the development of modern Macedonian poetry. Racin's poetry captured the essence of the Macedonian people's struggles and aspirations, and he became a voice for the national awakening and cultural identity of North Macedonia. His collection of poems, "White Dawns," remains a significant literary work, celebrated for its lyrical beauty, emotional depth, and social consciousness.

Dimitar Miladinov (1810-1862) and Konstantin Miladinov (1830-1862) - The Miladinov brothers were influential figures in the Macedonian national revival movement. They dedicated themselves to collecting and preserving Macedonian folklore and poetry, which played a crucial role in shaping the Macedonian national consciousness. Their extensive collection of folk songs, known as "The Collection of Macedonian Folk Songs," provides valuable insight into the rich cultural heritage and traditions of the Macedonian people.

Nikola Karev (1877-1905) - Nikola Karev was a revolutionary and a leader of the Internal Macedonian Revolutionary Organization (IMRO). He played a vital role in the fight for Macedonian independence from the Ottoman Empire. Karev organized and led numerous uprisings and resistance movements, aiming to secure autonomy and self-determination for the Macedonian people. His bravery and dedication to the cause have made him a symbol of the struggle for Macedonian independence and national identity.

Kiro Gligorov (1917-2012) - Kiro Gligorov was the first President of the Republic of Macedonia and played a significant role in the country's political development. He led North Macedonia through its independence process after the dissolution of Yugoslavia and played a crucial role in establishing the country's political institutions. Gligorov's leadership was marked by his commitment to promoting stability, democracy, and regional cooperation. His diplomatic efforts contributed to the recognition and integration of North Macedonia into the international community.

Vanco Mihajlov (1902-1990) - Vanco Mihajlov was a renowned painter and one of the founders of modern Macedonian art. Born in the village of Galichnik, Mihajlov's artistic journey was influenced by the rich natural landscapes and rural life of Macedonia. He played a significant role in shaping the development of Macedonian art in the early 20th century. Mihajlov's paintings captured the essence of the Macedonian countryside, depicting scenes of pastoral life, folklore, and traditions. His artwork showcased a unique blend of realism and symbolic expressionism, with a focus on capturing the spiritual and emotional essence of his subjects. Mihajlov's contributions to the art world have left a lasting impact on the cultural heritage of North Macedonia.

Gjorge Ivanov (1960-present) - Gjorge Ivanov served as the fifth President of North Macedonia from 2009 to 2019. A renowned academic and politician, Ivanov played a significant role in the country's political development during his two terms. As President, he focused on strengthening North Macedonia's international standing, promoting regional cooperation, and advocating for the country's NATO and EU integration. Ivanov's presidency coincided with crucial moments in North Macedonia's history, including the Prespa Agreement that resolved the long-standing name dispute with Greece. His leadership and diplomatic efforts played a role in fostering stability and progress in the country.

Dimitar Vlahov (1877-1953) - Dimitar Vlahov was a prominent writer, politician, and activist. He contributed significantly to the development of the Macedonian literary and cultural scene in the early 20th century. Vlahov was an advocate for the recognition of the Macedonian language and identity. He played a vital role in the publication of the first Macedonian grammar book and contributed to the standardization of the Macedonian language. As a politician, Vlahov actively participated in the Macedonian national movement and worked towards national and cultural autonomy for the Macedonian people.

Blaže Koneski (1921-1993) - Blaže Koneski was a prominent linguist, poet, and translator who played a crucial role in standardizing the Macedonian language. He was instrumental in establishing the Macedonian literary language and contributed significantly to the development of Macedonian literature. Koneski's literary works explored various themes, including love, nature, and patriotism. He also translated numerous literary works into Macedonian, introducing international literature to the Macedonian audience. Koneski's scholarly contributions, poetry, and translations have had a lasting impact on the Macedonian language and literature, solidifying his position as a key figure in the country's cultural and linguistic heritage.

2. Top Attractions in Skopje

Skopje offers a diverse range of attractions that captivate travelers. Explore the ancient ruins of Skopje Fortress and the architectural splendor of the Stone Bridge. Immerse yourself in the lively ambiance of the Old Bazaar and discover the rich cultural heritage it holds. Marvel at the colossal statue of Alexander the Great in Macedonia Square and delve into the city's past at the Skopje City Museum. From the Skopje Aqueduct to the Museum of Contemporary Art, each attraction is a piece of the tapestry that makes Skopje so captivating. Whether you're a history enthusiast, an art lover, or a nature enthusiast, Skopje's attractions promise a captivating and memorable journey through this enchanting city.

2.1 Skopje Fortress (Kale)

https://www.gettyimages.com/detail/photo/skopje-fortress-royalty-free-image/974453834?adppopup=true

Perched on a hill overlooking the city, Skopje Fortress, also known as Kale, is a must-visit attraction for history enthusiasts. Dating back to the 6th century, this ancient fortress offers a glimpse into Skopje's past. Visitors can explore its stone walls, towers, and archaeological exhibits, which showcase artifacts from different historical periods. The fortress also provides stunning panoramic views of Skopje, making it a perfect spot for photography and enjoying the city's skyline.

2.2 Stone Bridge

The Stone Bridge is an iconic symbol of Skopje, connecting the old and new parts of the city across the Vardar River. Constructed during the Ottoman period, this historic bridge is a popular gathering place for locals and visitors alike. Strolling across the bridge offers scenic views of the river, surrounding architecture, and the picturesque old bazaar. Illuminated at night, the Stone Bridge creates a magical ambiance and serves as a focal point for various cultural events and festivals.

2.3 Old Bazaar (Stara Čaršija)

https://www.gettyimages.com/detail/photo/street-in-the-old-bazaar-of-skopje-royalty-free-image/542236414?adppopup=true

One of the oldest and largest bazaars in the Balkans, the Old Bazaar is a vibrant and bustling district filled with narrow cobblestone streets, traditional Ottoman-era buildings, and a myriad of shops and cafes. The bazaar preserves Skopje's rich cultural heritage and offers a unique shopping experience, with merchants selling handicrafts, textiles, spices, and traditional souvenirs. Exploring the maze-like streets, visitors can discover historic mosques, caravanserais, and hammams, immersing themselves in the enchanting ambiance of this historical quarter.

2.4 Macedonia Square

Located in the heart of the city, Macedonia Square is a vibrant and bustling plaza that serves as a central gathering point for locals and tourists. The square is adorned with grand architecture, including the Macedonian National Theatre, Archaeological Museum, and numerous statues and fountains. The imposing statue of Alexander the Great stands at the center, symbolizing Skopje's ancient roots. Surrounded by shops, cafes, and the main pedestrian street, the square is a lively hub of activity and a starting point for exploring the city.

2.5 Skopje City Museum

Housed in the historic Old Railway Station building, the Skopje City Museum offers a comprehensive exploration of Skopje's history, culture, and art. The museum's exhibits cover various periods, from ancient civilizations to the Ottoman era and the modern age. Visitors can discover archaeological artifacts, ethnographic displays, and artworks that provide insights into the city's past. The museum also hosts temporary exhibitions and cultural events, making it a dynamic space for learning and appreciation of Skopje's heritage.

2.6 Skopje Aqueduct

The Skopje Aqueduct is a fascinating historical site located on the outskirts of the city. Although not as intact as it once was, the remaining arches of this ancient Roman aqueduct provide a glimpse into the city's past. It's an ideal spot for history enthusiasts and photographers looking to capture the juxtaposition of ancient ruins against the natural surroundings.

2.7 Museum of Contemporary Art

Situated on the edge of Skopje's City Park, the Museum of Contemporary Art showcases the works of Macedonian artists and international contemporary art exhibitions. The museum features a diverse range of artistic mediums, including paintings, sculptures, installations, and multimedia presentations. Art enthusiasts and those interested in contemporary culture will appreciate the thought-provoking exhibits and the opportunity to engage with the local art scene.

2.8 Memorial House of Mother Teresa

Skopje is the birthplace of Mother Teresa, and the Memorial House pays tribute to her life and humanitarian work. Visitors can explore the exhibits showcasing personal artifacts, photographs, and documents related to her extraordinary journey. The memorial offers insights into the life and legacy of one of the world's most revered humanitarians and provides a reflective space for contemplation.

2.9 Church of St. Clement of Ohrid

Located within the Skopje Fortress, the Church of St. Clement of Ohrid is an exquisite example of Byzantine architecture. Dating back to the 13th century, this small church is adorned with stunning frescoes, intricate woodwork, and religious icons. It offers a serene and contemplative atmosphere, allowing visitors to appreciate the artistry and spirituality of this historic religious site.

2.10 Skopje City Park

Skopje City Park, also known as **Gradski Park**, is a green oasis in the heart of the city. Spanning over 200 hectares, it provides a peaceful retreat from the urban bustle. The park offers picturesque walking paths, lush gardens, and recreational facilities, making it an ideal place for leisurely strolls, picnics, and outdoor activities. The park also houses several monuments and statues, adding to its cultural and historical significance.

3. When to Visit Skopje

The ideal time to visit Skopje largely depends on your personal preferences and the experiences you seek. Skopje experiences a moderate continental climate, with distinct seasons throughout the year. Here are some insights to help you plan your visit:

Spring (April to June)

Spring in Skopje is a delightful season when the city awakens from the winter slumber. As the temperatures gradually rise, Skopje becomes adorned with vibrant colors and blossoming flowers. The parks and gardens come to life, offering a picturesque setting for leisurely walks and picnics. The City Park and Gradski Trgovski Park are particularly enchanting during this time, with their lush greenery and fragrant blooms.

With temperatures ranging from around 15°C to 25°C (59°F to 77°F), it's an ideal time to explore Skopje's outdoor attractions, such as the Stone Bridge and the scenic Vardar River. Spring is also a great time to discover the rich history and cultural heritage of Skopje by visiting landmarks like the Skopje Fortress or exploring the Old Bazaar.

Summer (July to August)

Summer in Skopje (July to August) is characterized by long, sunny days and a vibrant city atmosphere. The temperatures often soar above 30°C (86°F), creating a lively and energetic ambiance. This is the perfect time to experience Skopje's vibrant street life, outdoor cafes, and bustling squares. Take a leisurely stroll along the Vardar River promenade or visit the iconic Macedonia Square, which becomes a hub of activity during the summer months.

Skopje's open-air events and festivals are also in full swing during this time, offering a chance to immerse yourself in the local culture and enjoy live music, performances, and traditional food. Don't miss the opportunity to explore the Old Bazaar, a labyrinth of narrow streets lined with shops, restaurants, and centuries-old mosques. With the longer daylight hours, you'll have plenty of time to make the most of Skopje's vibrant summer scene.

Autumn (September to November)

Autumn (September to November) in Skopje brings a gentle transition from the summer heat to cooler temperatures and a kaleidoscope of colors. The cityscape is adorned with the warm hues of autumn foliage, creating a picturesque setting. As the temperatures range from around 10°C to 20°C (50°F to 68°F), it's a comfortable time to explore Skopje's outdoor attractions and enjoy leisurely walks.

The Matka Canyon, just a short drive from the city, is particularly stunning during this season, with its towering cliffs and vibrant foliage reflected in the crystal-clear waters of the Treska River. Autumn is also a great time to savor traditional Macedonian cuisine, with hearty dishes like gravče na tavče (baked beans) and ajvar (roasted red pepper spread) taking center stage. Be sure to explore Skopje's vibrant culinary scene and indulge in the flavors of the season.

Winter (December to February)

Winter in Skopje (December to February) brings a magical ambiance to the city. The temperatures drop, and occasional snowfall covers the streets, parks, and surrounding mountains. Skopje's winter landscapes, including the Stone Bridge and the Skopje Fortress, are transformed into a winter wonderland, exuding charm and tranquility.

The city takes on a festive spirit during the Christmas season, with decorations, markets, and ice skating rinks adding to the enchantment. This is also the time to indulge in warm comfort foods like sarma (cabbage rolls) and tavče gravče (baked beans), which are popular during the winter months. While temperatures range from around -5°C to 5°C (23°F to 41°F), the chilly weather offers the perfect excuse to cozy up in cafes and enjoy hot beverages like traditional Turkish coffee or warm rakija (fruit brandy). Skopje's winter atmosphere is truly magical, offering a unique experience for visitors seeking a wintertime getaway.

It's worth noting that Skopje can be visited throughout the year, as each season offers its own charm and unique experiences. Consider your preferred weather, outdoor activities, and any specific events or festivals you'd like to witness when deciding the best time to visit. Remember to check the local weather forecast and consider booking accommodations and attractions in advance, especially during peak tourist seasons.

FAQs: Traveling to Skopje

Here are some frequently asked questions (FAQs) about visiting Skopje along with their answers:

Is Skopje a safe city to visit?

Skopje is generally a safe city for tourists. Like any other destination, it's advisable to take normal precautions such as staying aware of your surroundings, keeping valuables secure, and using licensed taxis or transportation services. As with any travel, it's a good idea to have travel insurance that covers medical emergencies and trip cancellations.

What currency is used in Skopje, and are credit cards widely accepted?

The official currency of North Macedonia is the Macedonian Denar (MKD). While cash is widely accepted, credit cards are also commonly used in hotels, restaurants, and larger establishments. It's advisable to carry some local currency for smaller establishments, local markets, and public transportation.

Do I need a visa to visit Skopje?

Visa requirements for Skopje depend on your nationality. Citizens of certain countries may require a visa, while others can enter visa-free or receive a visa on arrival. It's recommended to check the visa requirements specific to your country of citizenship well in advance of your trip. Contact the nearest Macedonian embassy or consulate for the most up-to-date information.

What language is spoken in Skopje?

The official language of North Macedonia is Macedonian, but the presence of a sizable Albanian community means that the Albanian language also holds official status in certain regions, including parts of Skopje. Both Macedonian and Albanian are commonly spoken and understood in Skopje, reflecting the city's linguistic diversity. English is also widely spoken, particularly in tourist areas, hotels, and restaurants, making it easy for visitors to communicate and navigate their way through the city.

What are the transportation options in Skopje?

Skopje has a well-developed transportation system. The city offers buses, taxis, and ride-sharing services like Uber. The public transportation network includes buses and a recently introduced subway system. Taxis are also readily available, and it's advisable to use licensed taxis or request a ride through a reputable mobile app.

Are there any cultural customs or etiquette I should be aware of?

Macedonian culture is known for its warmth and hospitality. It's appreciated to greet locals with a friendly "Dobar den" (Good day) and show respect for cultural norms. When visiting churches or monasteries, modest dress is expected, covering shoulders and knees. It's also customary to remove shoes before entering someone's home.

4. Getting to Skopje

4.1 Flights and Airports

Skopje is conveniently connected to many global destinations, primarily in Europe, with increasing connectivity to other continents as well.

Skopje International Airport (SKP), also known as Alexander the Great Airport, is the largest airport in North Macedonia and serves as the main gateway to Skopje. It's located about 20 kilometers southeast of Skopje city center.
Flights

Numerous airlines offer services to Skopje, including traditional carriers such as **Turkish Airlines, Austrian Airlines**, and **Lufthansa**, as well as budget airlines such as **Wizz Air**. Wizz Air has a large presence at Skopje airport, offering cheap flights to numerous destinations across Europe.

For the best fares and flight options, use flight comparison websites like **Skyscanner** (www.skyscanner.com) or **Expedia** (www.expedia.com). Also, do remember to check the airlines' official websites, as they may have special promotions not listed on comparison sites.

The prices for flights to Skopje vary greatly depending on your departure location and the time of booking. As a general rule, it's advisable to **book your flight tickets well in advance** to get the best deals.

Airport to City Center

Upon arrival, there are several options to reach the city center from the Skopje International Airport.

1. Taxi: The most convenient, albeit more expensive, option is to take a taxi. It costs around €20 to €25 for a trip from the airport to the city center. Make sure to agree on the price before getting into the taxi to avoid overcharging.

2. Bus: The cheaper option is the bus. **Vardar Express** operates a shuttle bus service between the airport and the city center, with tickets costing around €3. You can find more information on their website (www.vardarexpress.com).

3. Car Rental: If you plan to explore more of North Macedonia during your stay, you may consider renting a car. Several car rental services like **Europcar**, **Hertz**, and **Sixt** are available at the airport. Booking online in advance usually gives you a better rate.

4. Private Transfer: If you prefer a hassle-free ride, you can pre-book a private transfer service. Companies like **Welcome Pickups** (www.welcomepickups.com) provide reliable and personalized airport pickup services.

Remember, if you're not a citizen of the European Union, you may need a visa to enter North Macedonia. Make sure to check the visa requirements before planning your journey.

4.2 Bus Connections

There are several bus companies operating in Skopje, offering a wide range of routes and schedules. Some of the prominent bus companies include **Matpu, Eurolines, and Simeonidis Tours,** among others. These companies provide regular services connecting Skopje to various destinations in the region, including cities in Albania, Serbia, Bulgaria, Greece, Kosovo, and other countries in the Balkans.

Traveling by bus to Skopje offers flexibility and affordability, allowing you to enjoy scenic landscapes and explore different regions along the way. The buses are typically comfortable and equipped with amenities like air conditioning and Wi-Fi, ensuring a pleasant journey. The duration of the bus trip varies depending on the distance and the specific route, but buses generally provide a convenient option for traveling to Skopje.

Tickets for bus travel can be purchased in advance online, at the bus station ticket counters, or sometimes directly from the bus driver, depending on availability. It's advisable to check the bus schedules and book tickets in advance, especially during peak travel seasons.

Skopje's central bus station is well-connected to the city's public transportation network, making it easy to reach your accommodation or explore the city upon arrival. Taxis and ride-sharing services are also available outside the bus station for convenient transfers to your destination within Skopje.

Whether you are planning a short trip from a nearby city or embarking on a longer journey through the Balkans, bus connections provide a reliable and affordable means of reaching Skopje and discovering the cultural and historical treasures of the region.

4.3 Visa Requirements and Entry Regulations

Travelers planning to visit North Macedonia, including its capital Skopje, should familiarize themselves with the visa requirements and entry conditions. The specific visa regulations depend on the nationality of the visitor.

Visa-free entry: Citizens of certain countries are allowed to enter North Macedonia without a visa and stay for a specified period. For example, visitors from the European Union (EU), the United States, Canada, Australia, New Zealand, and many other countries can enter for up to 90 days within a 180-day period without a visa. It's essential to check the official government sources or contact the nearest Macedonian embassy or consulate to confirm the visa requirements based on your nationality.

Visa on arrival: Some nationalities that do not have visa-free access to North Macedonia may be eligible for a visa on arrival. This option allows travelers to obtain a visa upon arrival at the airport or border checkpoint. However, it's advisable to check if this option is available and ensure you meet the specific requirements and have the necessary documents, such as a valid passport, proof of accommodation, and sufficient funds.

Visa application: Visitors from countries that require a visa for entry into North Macedonia should apply for a visa in advance through the nearest Macedonian embassy or consulate. The application process typically includes submitting the required documents, such as a completed application form, passport photos, valid passport, travel itinerary, proof of accommodation, financial means, and any other specific documents requested by the embassy or consulate. It's recommended to apply for a visa well in advance of your planned trip to allow for sufficient processing time.

It's important to note that visa regulations and entry requirements can change, so it's always advisable to check the latest information provided by the Ministry of Foreign Affairs of North Macedonia or consult with the appropriate embassy or consulate before traveling. Additionally, ensure that your passport has a validity of at least six months beyond your planned departure date from North Macedonia.

5. Getting Around Skopje

Skopje offers a variety of transportation options, allowing both residents and tourists to navigate the city with ease.

Here's an overview of the best ways to get around the city:

5.1 Public Transport
Buses are the primary mode of public transportation in Skopje. The city's bus system is managed by **JSP Skopje**. Tickets cost about €0.70 if bought at kiosks, and €1.00 if bought on the bus. Day, three-day, and week passes are available for frequent travelers and can be purchased at JSP offices or online at the **JSP website** (www.jsp.com.mk). Buses are generally reliable, but can be crowded during rush hour.

5.2 Taxis
Taxis are quite affordable in Skopje and offer a convenient way to travel around the city, especially if you're in a hurry or carrying heavy luggage. Most taxis operate with a meter, and a short trip within the city center typically costs around €2-€3. Some popular taxi companies include **Deana Taxi**, **Balkan Taxi**, and **Global Taxi**.

5.3 Car Rental
If you prefer to have your own transport, consider renting a car. Companies such as **Europcar**, **Hertz**, and **Sixt** have branches in the city. Remember that driving in Skopje requires a valid international driver's license. Also, take note that parking in the city center can be challenging due to the limited availability of parking spaces.

5.4 Bicycles

Skopje is becoming more bike-friendly with an increasing number of bike lanes. The city operates a **public bike rental system** known as **Skopje Bike**, allowing you to rent a bicycle for a small fee. This is a great option if you're looking to explore the city at your own pace and get some exercise along the way. More information about this can be found on their website (www.skopjebike.mk).

5.5 Walking

Many of Skopje's main attractions are located close together, particularly in the city center, which makes **walking** an excellent option. The city is full of pedestrian zones and picturesque bridges crossing the Vardar River, connecting the old bazaar area with the main square and city park.

Remember: Always stay safe while navigating the city. Keep an eye on traffic signs and signals, and be aware of your belongings at all times. Skopje is generally a safe city, but like any other destination, it's essential to stay vigilant.

6. Where to Stay in Skopje

There's a wide range of accommodation options in Skopje, with choices to suit every traveler's needs and preferences. Whether you're seeking luxury hotels, boutique stays, or budget-friendly hostels, Skopje has it all. Here are some of the best hotels and hostels in the city that provide excellent amenities, convenient locations, and a memorable stay.

6.1 Best Hotels in Skopje

Good hotel choices in Skopje include international brands such as Marriott as well as the local Hotel Aleksandar Palace.

6.1.1 Hotel Marriott Skopje

Hotel Marriott Skopje is a haven of luxury in the bustling heart of Skopje. Each of its elegantly designed rooms is equipped with plush bedding, spacious bathrooms, high-speed internet, and a flat-screen TV, offering an optimum level of comfort. For prices starting at around €130 per night, guests can also enjoy a range of on-site facilities such as a state-of-the-art fitness center, indulgent spa, and a heated indoor pool. Food lovers will delight in the hotel's diverse dining options, including international cuisine at the Distrikt Bar and Kitchen and spectacular panoramic views of Skopje's skyline at the Vista Rooftop Lounge. More details are available on their official website (www.marriott.com/hotels/travel/skpmd-skopje-marriott-hotel/).

6.1.2 Hotel Aleksandar Palace

Perched on the banks of the Vardar River, the **Hotel Aleksandar Palace** is an exceptional blend of picturesque location and superb service. Rooms are spacious, tastefully decorated, and start at approximately €90 per night. Each room is well-equipped with a cozy ambiance and modern amenities, ensuring a relaxing stay. The hotel boasts a sparkling outdoor pool, a comprehensive wellness center, and a lively casino for entertainment. Gastronomy lovers will appreciate the delectable Macedonian and international dishes served at the hotel's restaurant. For more information, visit their website (www.aleksandarpalace.com.mk).

6.1.3 Hotel Super 8
For those seeking modern comfort without breaking the bank, the **Hotel Super 8** is the perfect choice. Rooms start at around €40 per night and are well-appointed with air conditioning, flat-screen TVs, and private bathrooms. Guests can also enjoy a complimentary breakfast and free Wi-Fi throughout the hotel. Its central location, just a stone's throw from Skopje's main attractions and vibrant nightlife, makes it incredibly convenient for exploring the city. Check out their website for more details (www.hotelsuper8.com).

6.1.4 Hotel Solun
Hotel Solun, a boutique hotel nestled in Skopje's historic Old Bazaar, blends contemporary design with traditional charm. With prices starting from around €70 per night, each stylish room features elegant decor, comfortable furnishings, and modern amenities. The hotel boasts a rooftop terrace that offers panoramic city views and a chic bar serving a wide variety of drinks. The location is ideal for those keen on immersing themselves in historic sites,

exploring local markets, and trying authentic Macedonian cuisine. Visit their official website for more details (www.hotelsolun.mk).

6.1.5 Hotel Park Skopje
Just a short walk from the city park and the main square, **Hotel Park Skopje** provides a serene retreat in the vibrant city. With rooms starting from €50 per night, guests can enjoy spacious and comfortable accommodations equipped with modern amenities. The hotel offers several relaxing spaces including a peaceful garden and a terrace bar, perfect for unwinding after a day of exploration. Its friendly staff, coupled with its convenient location, make Hotel Park an ideal choice for both leisure and business travelers. For more information, visit their website (www.hotelpark.com.mk).

6.2 Best Hostels in Skopje

6.2.1 Shanti Hostel

Shanti Hostel, located in the heart of Skopje, provides a cozy and sociable atmosphere for travelers. The hostel offers a variety of room options, including dormitories and private rooms, all equipped with comfortable beds and lockers. Guests can relax in the communal lounge, mingle with fellow travelers, or enjoy a refreshing drink at the on-site bar. The hostel also organizes social events and tours to help guests explore Skopje and its surroundings.

6.2.2 Hostel Valentin

Situated in a historic building in Skopje's Old Town, Hostel Valentin exudes charm and character. The hostel offers clean and comfortable dormitory rooms with shared bathrooms. Guests can relax in the courtyard or socialize in the communal lounge. The friendly staff is always ready to provide helpful tips and recommendations for exploring the city. The hostel's prime location allows easy access to the main attractions, restaurants, and nightlife.

6.2.3 Unity Hostel

With its welcoming and vibrant atmosphere, Unity Hostel is a popular choice among backpackers and budget travelers. The hostel features dormitory rooms with cozy beds and individual lockers. Guests can enjoy the communal kitchen, common area, and outdoor terrace. The hostel organizes pub crawls and city tours, providing opportunities for guests to socialize and explore Skopje together.

6.2.4 Get Inn Skopje Hostel

Get Inn Skopje Hostel offers a comfortable and affordable stay in the city center. The hostel provides well-designed dormitory rooms with modern amenities and individual lockers. Guests can relax in the common lounge, prepare meals in the shared kitchen, or enjoy a game of billiards. The hostel's friendly staff is always available to assist with travel arrangements and offer local insights.

6.2.5 Urban Hostel & Apartments

Conveniently located near Skopje's main bus and train station, Urban Hostel & Apartments is a popular choice for budget travelers. The hostel offers dormitory rooms and private apartments with shared or private bathrooms. Guests can socialize in the common lounge, cook in the fully equipped kitchen, or relax on the rooftop terrace. The hostel's friendly staff and relaxed atmosphere create a welcoming environment for all guests.

Skopje provides a diverse range of accommodation options, from luxury hotels to budget-friendly hostels, ensuring that every traveler can find a suitable place to stay. Whether you prefer a central location, scenic views, or a sociable atmosphere, these top hotels and hostels in Skopje offer excellent amenities, comfortable rooms, and convenient access to the city's attractions.

7. Dining and Cuisine in Skopje

From traditional Macedonian dishes to international flavors, Skopje provides a wide range of dining options to satisfy every palate. Whether you're seeking authentic local cuisine, exploring unique culinary experiences, or indulging in international flavors, Skopje has something to offer for every food lover. Embark on a gastronomic journey as we explore the dining and cuisine in Skopje, highlighting traditional Macedonian foods, recommended restaurants, vegetarian and vegan options, as well as the vibrant café and coffee shop culture.

7.1 Traditional Macedonian Foods

Macedonian cuisine is a delightful blend of Mediterranean, Balkan, and Middle Eastern influences, offering a unique culinary experience for visitors. Traditional Macedonian foods showcase the country's rich history and diverse cultural heritage. From hearty stews to savory grilled meats and refreshing salads, Macedonian cuisine is a celebration of flavors and traditions passed down through generations.

Tavche Gravche

One of the most iconic dishes in Macedonian cuisine is **Tavche Gravche.** This traditional bean stew is made with baked beans, onions, red pepper, and a medley of aromatic spices. The dish is slow-cooked to perfection, resulting in a rich and creamy texture with a depth of flavors. Tavche Gravche is often served with freshly baked bread, creating a comforting and satisfying meal that warms both the body and soul.

Another beloved Macedonian dish is Ajvar, a vibrant relish made from roasted red peppers, eggplant, garlic, and olive oil. Ajvar bursts with smoky and tangy flavors, offering a delightful balance of sweetness and acidity. It is often enjoyed as a spread on bread or as a side dish with grilled meats. The versatility of Ajvar makes it a staple in Macedonian households, and it embodies the country's love for fresh and bold flavors.

When it comes to grilled meats, Kebapi takes center stage. These small and seasoned meat sausages are a popular street food in Macedonia. Made from a mixture of beef and lamb, Kebapi are grilled to perfection, resulting in juicy and flavorful bites. They are often served with flatbread, onions, and a dollop of creamy yogurt, adding a refreshing element to the dish. Kebapi are a true delight for meat lovers, and their distinct taste showcases the mastery of Macedonian grilling techniques.

For a taste of Macedonian pizza, Pastrmajlija is a must-try. This oval-shaped dish resembles a pizza but is uniquely Macedonian. It is topped with chunks of marinated and pan-fried pork, which infuses the dough with its savory flavors. The dough is typically thin and crispy, providing a delightful contrast to the tender and flavorful pork. Pastrmajlija is a regional specialty, particularly popular in the city of Ohrid, and it is often enjoyed with a glass of Macedonian wine, further enhancing the dining experience.

https://www.gettyimages.com/detail/photo/shopska-salad-in-macedonia-royalty-free-image/1040407636?adppopup=true

No exploration of Macedonian cuisine is complete without indulging in a refreshing **Shopska Salad**. This vibrant salad features a combination of fresh ingredients, including chopped tomatoes, cucumbers, onions, and peppers. It is then generously topped with grated white cheese, usually made from sheep's milk. The salad is dressed with a drizzle of olive oil and a splash of vinegar, creating a light and tangy flavor profile. Shopska Salad not only delights the palate but also showcases the abundance of fresh produce that Macedonia has to offer.

In addition to these traditional dishes, Macedonian cuisine is known for its use of locally sourced ingredients, such as dairy products, fresh vegetables, and aromatic herbs. The country's diverse landscape, ranging from fertile valleys to mountainous regions, provides an abundance of agricultural treasures that contribute to the richness and variety of Macedonian cuisine.

Another iconic dish is **Burek**, a beloved pastry that holds a special place in the hearts and stomachs of Macedonians. Burek is a flaky and savory pie made with layers of thin phyllo dough filled with various fillings, most commonly cheese, meat, or spinach. It is a staple dish in Macedonian cuisine and is often enjoyed as a hearty breakfast or a satisfying snack throughout the day.

https://www.gettyimages.com/detail/photo/turkish-pastry-royalty-free-image/169982759?adppopup=true

The layers of delicate phyllo dough create a crispy texture, while the flavorful fillings provide a burst of savory goodness. Burek is typically enjoyed with a side of plain yogurt, which complements the richness of the pastry and adds a creamy and tangy element to the overall taste. Another delightful treat is **Ajvar Rolls,** a delicious twist on the traditional Ajvar relish.

Ajvar Rolls

In Macedonia, they make Ajvar Rolls by spreading a generous amount of Ajvar on a thin sheet of dough and rolling it into a cylindrical shape. The rolls are then baked until golden and crispy, resulting in a delightful combination of flavors and textures. The outer layer of the rolls is flaky and crunchy, while the Ajvar filling infuses each bite with its smoky and tangy notes. Ajvar Rolls are often enjoyed as a snack or appetizer, showcasing the versatility and creativity of Macedonian cuisine.

When it comes to sweet indulgences, Macedonian cuisine offers a delightful range of desserts. One such treat is Tulumba, a traditional deep-fried pastry similar to churros. These elongated and syrup-soaked pastries are made by piping a dough mixture into hot oil, resulting in crispy and golden tubes. Once fried, Tulumba are soaked

65

in a sweet syrup made from sugar, water, and lemon juice, infusing them with a delectable sweetness. These syrup-drenched delights are often served cold, providing a refreshing and satisfying dessert option.

7.2 Recommended Restaurants

Equilibrium
Nestled in the heart of Skopje's city center, Equilibrium restaurant offers a fine dining experience that combines elegant ambiance with exquisite flavors. The restaurant prides itself on its innovative and creative approach to Macedonian cuisine, showcasing the best of local ingredients in unique and imaginative dishes. Equilibrium's menu features a fusion of traditional Macedonian flavors with contemporary twists, resulting in a culinary journey that surprises and delights the taste buds.

Zanzibar Restaurant
Located near the Macedonian Square, Zanzibar Restaurant is a trendy and contemporary dining establishment that offers a fusion of international flavors. The restaurant's stylish and modern decor sets the stage for a memorable dining experience. The menu features a diverse selection of dishes influenced by Mediterranean, Asian, and Middle Eastern cuisines. From fresh seafood and sushi to gourmet burgers and exotic salads, Zanzibar Restaurant caters to a wide range of tastes. The attentive staff and chic ambiance make it a popular choice for both locals and tourists looking for a sophisticated dining experience.

Destan

Destan is a charming restaurant situated in the heart of Skopje's Old Bazaar. With its rustic and traditional decor, it captures the essence of Macedonian culture and heritage. The menu focuses on authentic Macedonian dishes prepared with locally sourced ingredients. From hearty stews and grilled meats to traditional desserts, each dish reflects the rich flavors and traditions of Macedonian cuisine. The restaurant's warm and friendly atmosphere, combined with the delightful flavors of the food, create a memorable dining experience for visitors.

Taj Mahal
For those seeking a taste of exotic flavors, Taj Mahal is a must-visit restaurant in Skopje. Located near the Stone Bridge, this Indian restaurant offers an array of aromatic and flavorful dishes inspired by the rich culinary traditions of India. From fragrant curries and tandoori specialties to mouthwatering biryanis and naan bread, Taj Mahal takes diners on a culinary journey to the vibrant streets of India. The restaurant's colorful and vibrant interior, accompanied by attentive service, adds to the overall dining experience.

Amigos
Located in the heart of Skopje, Amigos is a popular restaurant that offers a fusion of Mexican and Balkan cuisine. The vibrant and colorful ambiance sets the stage for a memorable dining experience. The menu features a variety of dishes such as tacos, burritos, enchiladas, and sizzling fajitas, all prepared with fresh and high-quality ingredients. The flavors are authentic, and the portions are generous, making it a favorite spot for locals and tourists alike.

Old House

Situated in the charming Old Bazaar, Old House is a traditional Macedonian restaurant known for its warm and cozy atmosphere. Housed in a beautifully restored Ottoman-era building, the restaurant offers a unique dining experience that combines history and gastronomy. The menu showcases a wide array of traditional Macedonian dishes, including grilled meats, hearty stews, and flavorful vegetable dishes. The use of local ingredients and traditional cooking techniques ensures an authentic taste of Macedonian cuisine.

Skopski Merak

Skopski Merak is a renowned restaurant that celebrates the rich culinary heritage of Skopje and the surrounding region. Located in the city center, the restaurant offers a rustic and inviting ambiance with traditional Macedonian decor. The menu features a wide range of traditional dishes, highlighting the flavors and techniques that have been passed down through generations. From sizzling kebabs to aromatic stews, every dish is a testament to the flavors and traditions of Macedonian cuisine.

Dal Met Fu

For those craving Italian cuisine, Dal Met Fu is the place to go. This stylish restaurant is known for its authentic Italian flavors and contemporary presentation. The menu boasts a variety of classic Italian dishes, including handmade pastas, wood-fired pizzas, and fresh seafood. The skilled chefs ensure that each dish is prepared with precision and attention to detail, resulting in a memorable dining experience. The restaurant also offers an extensive selection of Italian wines to complement the flavors of the dishes.

Kaj Serdarot

Kaj Serdarot is a charming restaurant located in the historic neighborhood of Debar Maalo. With its cozy and intimate setting, it provides a perfect atmosphere for a romantic dinner or a gathering with friends. The menu features a blend of Mediterranean and Balkan flavors, offering a unique twist on traditional Macedonian cuisine. From grilled meats to fresh seafood, each dish is prepared with care and creativity. The knowledgeable staff is always ready to recommend the perfect wine pairing to enhance your dining experience.

Restoran Pelister

Situated near the City Park, Restoran Pelister is a popular dining spot that offers a diverse menu inspired by both Macedonian and international cuisines. The restaurant's spacious terrace provides a picturesque setting for outdoor dining during the warmer months, while the cozy interior is perfect for a cozy meal during winter. The menu features a wide range of dishes, from juicy steaks and seafood delicacies to vegetarian options and hearty salads. The friendly service and welcoming atmosphere make Restoran Pelister a favorite among locals and visitors alike.

Casa Mia

Casa Mia is a hidden gem tucked away in the peaceful neighborhood of Karposh. This family-owned restaurant is known for its warm hospitality and homestyle cooking. The menu features a mix of Macedonian and European dishes, showcasing the chef's culinary expertise and creativity. From traditional Macedonian specialties to modern interpretations, every dish is prepared with love and attention to detail.

7.3 Vegetarian and Vegan Options

Skopje has seen a surge in the popularity of vegan and vegetarian lifestyles in recent years.

One of the standout vegan restaurants in Skopje is **"Vegehop,"** a cozy eatery that offers a diverse menu of vegan dishes inspired by international flavors. From vegan burgers and wraps to colorful salads and hearty soups, Vegehop creates culinary delights that satisfy both the taste buds and the conscience. The restaurant focuses on using fresh, locally sourced ingredients to ensure the highest quality and freshness of their dishes.

For those seeking a taste of traditional Macedonian cuisine with a vegan twist, **"Gostilnica Ima Da!"** is the place to be. This vegan-friendly restaurant takes traditional Macedonian dishes and reimagines them using plant-based ingredients. From vegan "kebapi" (grilled meat substitutes) and "tarator" (a refreshing yogurt-based soup) to vegan "baklava" (a sweet pastry), Gostilnica Ima Da! brings the rich flavors of Macedonian cuisine to the vegan table. The restaurant's commitment to preserving the authenticity of traditional dishes while offering vegan alternatives has earned it a loyal following among locals and visitors alike.

Skopje also boasts a number of vegetarian-friendly restaurants that cater to those who choose to include dairy and eggs in their diet. One such establishment is **"Halo,"** a popular vegetarian restaurant known for its extensive menu of vegetarian dishes with Mediterranean and international influences. From flavorful pasta dishes and creative salads to vegetarian versions of traditional Macedonian specialties, Halo provides a diverse array of options to satisfy vegetarian palates. The restaurant's inviting atmosphere and attentive service make it a favorite spot for both vegetarians and omnivores.

In addition to dedicated vegan and vegetarian restaurants, Skopje offers a range of mainstream eateries that include vegan and vegetarian options on their menus. These establishments recognize the growing demand for plant-based choices and strive to accommodate the diverse dietary needs of their patrons. From Italian and Mexican restaurants to Asian fusion and sushi joints, many places in Skopje are happy to customize dishes or offer specific vegan or vegetarian sections on their menus.

For a quick bite or a caffeine fix, Skopje's vegan and vegetarian-friendly cafes are worth a visit. **"The Green Mill"** is a charming cafe that offers a variety of vegan and vegetarian options, including sandwiches, wraps, and delectable desserts. The cafe's cozy atmosphere and welcoming staff make it an ideal spot to relax and enjoy a plant-based treat. **"Coffee Lab"** is another popular cafe that serves vegan and vegetarian beverages, including plant-based milk alternatives for coffee and tea. Whether you're looking for a refreshing smoothie, a flavorful herbal tea, or a creamy latte, Coffee Lab has something to satisfy your cravings.

7.4 Cafes and Coffee Shops

Skopje boasts a thriving cafe culture that is deeply ingrained in the city's social fabric. From traditional coffee houses to trendy modern cafes, Skopje offers a wide range of options for coffee lovers to indulge in their favorite brew. Let's delve into the rich coffee culture of Skopje and discover some of the best destinations for coffee enthusiasts in different neighborhoods.

Coffee holds a special place in Macedonian culture, and Skopje reflects this with its abundance of cafes that serve exceptional coffee. Traditional coffee houses, known as **"kafanas,"** are a significant part of the city's coffee culture. These establishments provide a unique experience where visitors can savor the traditional Macedonian way of enjoying coffee.

One such iconic kafana is **"Destan,"** located in the Old Bazaar neighborhood. With its historic ambiance, aromatic coffee, and friendly service, Destan takes you back in time while you sip on a cup of Turkish-style coffee and soak in the authentic atmosphere.

Moving into the modern era, Skopje offers a plethora of contemporary cafes that cater to diverse tastes and preferences. In the trendy Debar Maalo neighborhood, **"Public Room"** stands out as a popular destination for coffee aficionados. This stylish and artistic cafe combines a cozy interior with a relaxed outdoor seating area, making it a perfect spot to enjoy a cup of specialty coffee or indulge in a sweet treat. Public Room also hosts cultural events, exhibitions, and live performances, adding an extra touch of vibrancy to your coffee experience.

Another gem in Skopje's cafe scene is **"Kafeterija,"** situated in the bustling City Center. With its sleek and modern decor, Kafeterija offers a hip and contemporary ambiance for coffee lovers. The cafe features a wide selection of specialty coffees sourced from various regions around the world. From single-origin pour-overs to expertly crafted espresso-based drinks, Kafeterija aims to satisfy even the most discerning coffee connoisseurs. Pair your coffee with a delectable pastry or a light snack, and enjoy the trendy atmosphere of this popular coffee spot.

Skopje's cafe culture extends beyond the city center, with hidden gems waiting to be discovered in different neighborhoods. In the vibrant neighborhood of Karposh, **"Zegin Cafe"** stands out as a beloved local institution. Known for its cozy setting and friendly staff, Zegin Cafe offers a wide range of coffee options, including traditional Macedonian coffee, espresso-based drinks, and flavored lattes. This neighborhood favorite also serves a variety of delicious pastries and desserts, making it a great place to unwind and enjoy a moment of indulgence.

Venturing into the Karpos neighborhood, **"Coffee Factory"** captures the attention of coffee enthusiasts with its specialty brews and inviting ambiance. This specialty coffee shop takes pride in sourcing high-quality beans from around the world and carefully roasting them in-house to create exceptional flavors. Coffee Factory offers a diverse menu of brewing methods, such as Chemex, V60, and Aeropress, allowing coffee lovers to explore different brewing techniques and savor unique flavors. With its minimalist decor and dedicated baristas, **Coffee Factory** creates an immersive coffee experience for visitors.

Skopje's cafe culture is not limited to these specific destinations, as there are numerous other cafes throughout the city that deserve mention. From charming local cafes tucked away in residential neighborhoods to trendy establishments in bustling commercial areas, Skopje offers an abundance of options for every coffee enthusiast to discover and enjoy.

Whether you prefer the traditional ambiance of a kafana or the contemporary vibe of a modern cafe, Skopje's cafe culture has something to offer everyone. Take your time and immerse yourself in the rich flavors and aromas of Macedonian coffee.

8. Culture and Entertainment in Skopje

Skopje, the capital city of North Macedonia, is a vibrant hub of culture and entertainment. With a rich history and a diverse population, the city offers a wide range of cultural attractions and entertainment options for locals and visitors alike. From museums and art galleries to theaters and nightlife, Skopje has something for everyone. Immerse yourself in the city's cultural tapestry and explore the various avenues of entertainment it has to offer.

8.1 Museums and Art Galleries

Skopje is home to an impressive collection of museums and art galleries that showcase the region's rich cultural heritage and artistic expressions. The museums offer a glimpse into the city's history, archaeology, art, and ethnography, while the art galleries provide a platform for contemporary artists to exhibit their works. Here are some notable museums and art galleries to explore:

The Museum of Macedonian Struggle:

The **Museum of Macedonian Struggle** is a significant
cultural institution that serves as a testament to the
tumultuous history of Macedonia. Located in the heart of
Skopje, the museum presents an elaborate narration of the
struggle of the Macedonian people against Ottoman rule
and their journey towards independence.

This state-of-the-art facility covers an area of about
3,000 square meters, featuring more than 20 rooms filled
with impressive dioramas, lifelike wax figures, and a rich
collection of photographs, documents, weapons, and
personal items from this critical period of Macedonian
history. Each exhibit provides a vivid account of
significant events, influential figures, and the fight for
freedom, bringing Macedonia's complex past to life.

Highlights of the museum include the room dedicated to
the Ilinden Uprising of 1903, a key event in the
Macedonian resistance, and the room focusing on the
creation of the Macedonian state. An audio guide is
available to accompany you, providing comprehensive
information and historical context for each exhibit.

The museum is open every day except Monday, from 10:00 AM to 6:00 PM. The entrance fee is approximately €3 for adults, with discounts available for students, seniors, and groups. Guided tours are available in English, German, French, and Russian, but it's recommended to book these in advance.

Before visiting, it's essential to note that the museum presents history from a Macedonian perspective, which can be a contentious topic given the region's complex history. However, this provides an insightful look into the Macedonian perception of their past struggles and triumphs.

To plan your visit and learn more about the Museum of Macedonian Struggle, check out their official website http://www.mmb.org.mk/

Whether you're a history buff or a casual traveler looking to understand more about Macedonia's past, a visit to the Museum of Macedonian Struggle promises to be both educational and moving. This museum truly offers a unique opportunity to delve into the rich tapestry of Macedonia's history.

The Museum of Contemporary Art:

The **Museum of Contemporary Art** in Skopje is one of the most significant cultural institutions in North Macedonia. Perched on a hill overlooking the city from the area known as the Kale Fortress, the museum offers a comprehensive display of modern art as well as captivating views of Skopje's landscape.

Address: Samoilova, 1000 Skopje, North Macedonia
The museum was established in 1963 following the catastrophic earthquake that hit Skopje. Countries from all over the world donated artworks to help restore the cultural life of the city. The result is an impressive collection that spans the mid-20th century to the present, featuring works by both Macedonian and international artists.

The Museum of Contemporary Art covers an area of 5000 square meters, including exhibition rooms, video screening rooms, a library, and a lecture hall. The permanent collection houses around 3,000 works of painting, sculpture, graphics, drawings, and installations.

Some of the highlights include works by renowned artists such as Picasso, Lichtenstein, Calder, and many others.

Macedonian artists represented include Borka Lazeski, Dimitar Kondovski, and Petar Mazev, whose pieces provide an insight into the development of contemporary Macedonian art.

The museum is open Tuesday to Sunday from 10:00 AM to 6:00 PM, and the entrance fee is approximately €2 for adults, with discounts available for students and seniors. Be sure to check out the "Donaupark" exhibit, which features outdoor sculptures donated by international artists. On a sunny day, the park outside the museum is a perfect spot for a picnic with a view.

Visitors should check the museum's official website (www.msuskopje.org.mk) for information on current temporary exhibitions and events, which cover a wide range of themes and often include innovative and challenging works from contemporary artists around the world.

Visiting the Museum of Contemporary Art in Skopje provides a fascinating journey through the evolution of art in the second half of the 20th century, making it a must-see destination for art enthusiasts and curious travelers alike.

The National Gallery of Macedonia:

The **National Gallery of Macedonia** is one of the leading cultural institutions in the country, dedicated to the collection, preservation, study, and presentation of Macedonian visual arts.

Address: Mito Hadživasilev Jasmin bb, 1000 Skopje, North Macedonia

Situated within the Daut Pasha Hammam, an architectural monument from the Ottoman period, the gallery is as much a historical attraction as it is an artistic one. The historic setting provides a unique backdrop for the vast array of artworks displayed within its walls.

The gallery's extensive collection spans from the 14th century to the present day, offering an insightful exploration of Macedonian art history. With over 7,000 works in its collection, the National Gallery of Macedonia showcases a broad range of artistic styles and mediums, including paintings, sculptures, prints, drawings, photographs, and new media.

Several exhibits stand out as key attractions at the gallery. The collection of icons, dating from the 14th to the 19th century, provides a look into Macedonia's rich religious art tradition. In addition, the gallery's holdings of contemporary and modern art offer fascinating insight into the country's artistic development in the 20th and 21st centuries, featuring works by significant Macedonian artists such as Petar Hadzi Boskov, Borka Lazeski, and Dusko Temkov.

The National Gallery of Macedonia is open from Tuesday to Sunday, 10:00 AM to 6:00 PM. The entrance fee is approximately €2, and discounts are available for students, seniors, and groups.

Before you visit, it's worth checking out the gallery's official website (https://nationalgallery.mk/?lang=en) for information on current exhibitions and events. The gallery often hosts temporary exhibits, workshops, and lectures, highlighting diverse aspects of Macedonian and international visual art.

The National Gallery of Macedonia is a cultural gem that offers a unique opportunity to explore the rich tapestry of Macedonian art. Its collection, combined with its historic setting, make it a must-visit destination for art lovers and history buffs alike.

The Archaeological Museum of Macedonia:

The **Archaeological Museum of Macedonia** is a cornerstone of Macedonian heritage and culture, offering a captivating journey through the country's rich history.

Address: Kej Dimitar Vlahov 5, 1000 Skopje, North Macedonia

Housed in an impressive Neoclassical-style building along the banks of the Vardar River, the museum is home to a diverse collection that spans thousands of years, from prehistoric times to the late Middle Ages.

With more than 6,000 artifacts spread across three floors and 15 exhibition halls, the Archaeological Museum of Macedonia showcases the archaeological and historical wealth of the region. It offers visitors a unique opportunity to delve into the area's past civilizations, culture, and way of life.

Among its many exhibits, the museum is renowned for its extraordinary collection of prehistoric artifacts, the rich trove of ancient Greek and Roman artifacts including statues, coins, jewelry, and pottery, and its extensive collection of Byzantine and medieval art.
One must-see exhibit is the Lihnidos Treasure, an impressive collection of 4th-century silverware discovered in Ohrid. Equally fascinating is the early Christian room, with its mosaics and stone-carved monuments depicting scenes from the Old and New Testaments.

The museum is open from Tuesday to Sunday, from 10:00 AM to 6:00 PM. The entrance fee is approximately €3 for adults, with discounts available for students, seniors, and groups.

Before visiting, it's recommended to check out the museum's official website (www.amm.org.mk) for information on current exhibitions, guided tours, and educational workshops.

The Archaeological Museum of Macedonia is a treasure trove of ancient artifacts and a must-visit destination for anyone interested in archaeology and history. Its diverse and extensive collection ensures a fascinating experience for all visitors, providing invaluable insights into Macedonia's ancient past.

Daut Pasha Hamam Gallery: This unique art space is located in a historic Turkish bathhouse and hosts temporary art exhibitions, cultural events, and performances. It offers a fusion of contemporary art and traditional architecture.

8.2 Theaters and Performing Arts

Skopje has a thriving theater scene, offering a variety of performances ranging from classical plays to contemporary productions. The city is home to several theaters and performance venues that showcase local talent and host international acts. Immerse yourself in the world of performing arts by exploring these prominent theaters:

Macedonian National Theater
Positioned in the beating heart of Skopje, the **Macedonian National Theater** is the most prestigious and largest theater in the country. This iconic institution offers a rich program of performances, ranging from intense dramas to lyrical ballets, vibrant operas, and captivating musicals. For performance schedules, ticket prices, and other relevant information, you can visit their official website (www.mnt.mk). It is highly recommended to book tickets in advance due to the popularity of the shows.

Youth Cultural Center (MKC)
Acting as the vibrant cultural hub for Skopje's youth, the **Youth Cultural Center**, or **MKC**, hosts an eclectic program of events. From theater performances and film screenings to live music concerts and art exhibitions, MKC provides a dynamic platform for emerging artists and encourages creative expression. For information on upcoming events and booking details, visit their official website (www.mkc.mk).

Kino Kultura
Kino Kultura is an alternative cinema and cultural center that champions independent and art-house films from

around the globe. Beyond film screenings, it also hosts thought-provoking film festivals, interactive workshops, and engaging discussions. For film enthusiasts, Kino Kultura is a haven of cinematic treasures. For information on current screenings and events, you can visit their official website (www.kinokultura.org.mk).

Skopje Jazz Festival

The **Skopje Jazz Festival** is an annual celebration of jazz that attracts an impressive roster of local and international jazz musicians. Audiences are treated to soulful performances that stretch the boundaries of the genre. This event is a must-attend for music lovers and is usually held in October. For line-ups, ticket prices, and other festival details, visit the official website (www.skopjejazzfest.com.mk).

8.3 Nightlife in Skopje

Skopje's nightlife scene is vibrant and diverse, offering a range of venues to suit different tastes and preferences. Whether you're looking for a relaxed evening in a cozy bar or an energetic night of dancing at a club, Skopje has options to cater to every mood. Here are some popular nightlife destinations:

Colosseum Club

One of Skopje's largest and most popular nightclubs, **Colosseum Club** is known for its energetic atmosphere and live performances by local and international DJs. The club often hosts themed nights and exclusive parties. For more information about upcoming events, check out their website: www.colosseum.mk.

Address: Blvd. Jane Sandanski 51, Skopje 1000, North Macedonia

Epicentar

If you're a fan of electronic music, **Epicentar** is a must-visit. This club features top DJs spinning techno, house, and trance music until the early morning hours. With its underground vibes and quality music, it's a favorite among locals.
Address: Mitropolit Teodosij Gologanov 61, Skopje 1000, North Macedonia

Menada

For a more relaxed evening, head to **Menada**, a charming wine bar located in Skopje's Old Bazaar. Here, you can enjoy a wide selection of Macedonian wines in a cozy and historic setting. No website is available, but it's easy to find in the heart of the city's historic area.
Address: Old Bazaar, Skopje 1000, North Macedonia

Public Room

A versatile venue that offers a bit of everything, **Public Room** serves as a café, bar, art space, and concert venue. It's an excellent place to experience local live music, art exhibitions, or simply enjoy a drink. Their website (www.publicroom.mk) provides an up-to-date schedule of events.
Address: 50 Divizija 22, Skopje 1000, North Macedonia

Ibiza Club

For those who enjoy Latin rhythms, **Ibiza Club** offers salsa and bachata nights where you can dance the night away. It's a vibrant and friendly place that also offers dance

classes for beginners. Check their Facebook page for more information: www.facebook.com/IbizaClubSkopje.
Address: Bul. Jane Sandanski 71a, Skopje 1000, North Macedonia

Debar Maalo: This bohemian neighborhood is known for its lively atmosphere and numerous bars and pubs. It's a great place to enjoy a drink, socialize with locals and fellow travelers, and soak up the vibrant ambiance.

Shishko Pub: Situated in the Old Bazaar, Shishko Pub is a favorite among locals and visitors alike. With its cozy interior and outdoor seating, it offers a relaxed setting to enjoy a wide selection of craft beers and cocktails.

District Club: Located in the city center, District Club is a popular spot for dancing and live music. It features a spacious dance floor, top-notch sound system, and a lineup of local and international DJs.

Cocktail Bars in Skopje
Skopje is home to a diverse selection of cocktail bars, each offering an elegant atmosphere and a menu of brilliantly crafted cocktails. Ranging from the timeless classics to inventive, contemporary mixes, these establishments provide the perfect backdrop to unwind after a day of sightseeing.

Squeeze Me
Squeeze Me is a trendy cocktail bar that combines fresh ingredients with high-quality spirits to craft their innovative cocktails. The cozy and modern atmosphere of this bar is ideal for casual get-togethers.
Address: Petar Poparsov 2, Skopje 1000, North Macedonia

Public Room

Not only a vibrant live music venue, **Public Room** also boasts an extensive cocktail menu. Enjoy a creatively mixed drink in this stylish, multifunctional space.

Address: 50 Divizija 22, Skopje 1000, North Macedonia

Sky Bar

Located on the rooftop of the Marriott Hotel, the **Sky Bar** offers a wide array of cocktails along with an unbeatable view of Skopje's cityscape. It's the perfect place to sip on a cocktail while taking in the sights of the city.

Address: Plostad Makedonija 7, Skopje 1000, North Macedonia

Cultura Rooftop Bar

Another rooftop favorite is **Cultura Rooftop Bar**. As well as providing panoramic views of the city, it offers an impressive selection of cocktails in a laid-back, atmospheric setting.

Address: Leninova 79/1-3, Skopje 1000, North Macedonia

8.4 Shopping in Skopje

Skopje offers a diverse shopping experience, from modern shopping malls to traditional markets. Whether you're looking for designer brands, local handicrafts, or fresh produce, the city has something to cater to every shopper's needs. Here are some popular shopping destinations:

Skopje City Mall: This modern shopping mall is home to a wide range of international and local brands. It features fashion boutiques, electronics stores, beauty salons, and a variety of dining options.

Old Bazaar: The Old Bazaar is a bustling marketplace where you can find an array of traditional crafts, textiles, jewelry, spices, and souvenirs. Stroll through its narrow streets and soak up the lively atmosphere while browsing the unique offerings.

GTC Shopping Center: Located in the city center, the GTC Shopping Center is a popular destination for fashion enthusiasts. It houses a mix of international and local fashion brands, along with cafes and restaurants.

Bit Pazar: Known as the largest open-air market in Skopje, Bit Pazar is a vibrant place to experience the local culture and find fresh produce, dairy products, spices, and other food items.

8.5 Top Souvenirs from Skopje

When visiting Skopje, you might want to bring home a few mementos of your trip. Here are some of the top souvenirs that reflect the culture and heritage of Skopje and North Macedonia:

1. Traditional Macedonian Embroidery: Skopje is renowned for its traditional hand-embroidered textiles, which include tablecloths, napkins, and clothing. These intricate works of art are a beautiful representation of Macedonian craft traditions.

2. Macedonian Honey: North Macedonia is famous for its high-quality, flavorful honey, thanks to its diverse flora. Honey from the region makes a sweet and authentic gift to take back home.

3. Macedonian Wine: The country has a rich winemaking tradition, with excellent reds and whites produced in its many vineyards. A bottle of local wine, such as Vranec or Traminec, is a wonderful souvenir for any wine lover.

4. Macedonian Filigree Jewelry: This delicate and intricate form of jewelry-making has been a tradition in Skopje for centuries. Each piece, often made from silver or gold, is unique and skillfully crafted.

5. Rakija: This traditional Balkan brandy is a popular spirit in North Macedonia and comes in various flavors, including plum, grape, and apricot. Just make sure to pack it securely in your checked luggage!

6. Macedonian Spices: Ajvar, a flavorful relish made from red bell peppers and garlic, is a must-buy. Also, consider picking up some local spice mixes, like Vegeta, that are essential to Macedonian cuisine.

7. Traditional Macedonian Music: Local music CDs can be found in music stores around the city. It's a great way to take a piece of Macedonia's rich musical heritage home with you.

8. Macedonian Ceramics: The city of Skopje has a strong tradition of ceramic arts, with many studios selling handmade and hand-painted pieces. These make for a beautiful, one-of-a-kind gift or keepsake.

These items can be found in local markets, specialty stores, and even some supermarkets around Skopje. The Old Bazaar in Skopje is an excellent place to start your souvenir hunt!

9. Outdoor Activities in Skopje

Skopje is not only known for its cultural attractions but also offers a plethora of outdoor activities for nature enthusiasts and adventure seekers. From beautiful parks and gardens to hiking trails, a zoo, and thrilling adventure sports, Skopje provides a variety of options to explore and enjoy the great outdoors.

9.1 Parks and Gardens

Skopje boasts several parks and gardens, providing green spaces where visitors can relax, have a picnic, or engage in recreational activities. These parks offer a tranquil escape from the hustle and bustle of the city and provide opportunities to appreciate nature. Here are some notable parks and gardens in Skopje:

City Park (Gradski Park): Located in the city center, City Park is a popular destination for both locals and tourists. It features tree-lined paths, colorful flower beds, and open green spaces. Visitors can enjoy leisurely walks, rent bicycles, or simply relax on the benches.

Millennium Cross Park: Situated on the slopes of Mount Vodno, Millennium Cross Park offers stunning panoramic views of Skopje. The park is home to the iconic Millennium Cross, a symbol of the city. Visitors can hike or take a cable car to reach the top and enjoy the breathtaking vistas.

Kale Fortress Park: Positioned on a hill overlooking the city, Kale Fortress Park combines history with natural beauty. The park offers splendid views of Skopje's skyline and the Vardar River. Visitors can explore the fortress ruins, walk along the old city walls, and take in the scenic surroundings.

9.2 Hiking and Nature Trails

Skopje and its surrounding areas are a paradise for hiking enthusiasts, with a range of trails that cater to different fitness levels and preferences. These trails allow visitors to immerse themselves in the natural beauty of the region and enjoy invigorating outdoor adventures. Here are some popular hiking and nature trails near Skopje:

Matka Canyon: Located just outside Skopje, Matka Canyon offers a picturesque setting for hiking. The canyon is home to stunning rock formations, caves, and the Matka Lake. Visitors can explore the various hiking trails, visit the Vrelo Cave, and enjoy boat rides on the lake.

Mount Vodno: Rising above Skopje, Mount Vodno is a popular destination for hiking and nature lovers. It offers several trails that lead to the summit, where the Millennium Cross stands. The trails provide opportunities to enjoy panoramic views, encounter diverse flora and fauna, and experience the tranquility of the mountain.

Golem Grad (Snake Island): Situated in Lake Prespa, Golem Grad is a natural reserve that can be reached by boat from Skopje. The island is known for its biodiversity and serves as a nesting ground for various bird species. Hiking on the island allows visitors to appreciate the unspoiled natural environment and observe wildlife.

9.3 Skopje Zoo

Skopje Zoo is a popular attraction for families and animal enthusiasts. Located in the heart of the city, the zoo is home to a wide variety of animals from different parts of the world. Visitors can explore the well-maintained enclosures and observe animals such as lions, tigers, bears, monkeys, and various bird species. The zoo also offers educational programs and activities for children, making it an ideal destination for a fun and educational day out.

9.4 Adventure Sports

For those seeking adrenaline-pumping experiences, Skopje offers a range of adventure sports that cater to thrill-seekers. From water-based activities to outdoor adventures, there are plenty of options to get your heart racing. Here are some adventure sports activities to try in Skopje:

White-water Rafting: The Treska River, located near Skopje, provides excellent opportunities for white-water rafting. Adventurers can navigate the rapids and enjoy the excitement of this thrilling water sport while taking in the scenic beauty of the surrounding landscape.

Paragliding: Skopje's mountainous terrain and favorable wind conditions make it an ideal destination for paragliding. Adventure enthusiasts can soar through the skies, enjoying panoramic views of the city and its surroundings.

Rock Climbing: Skopje and its surrounding areas offer numerous rock climbing spots suitable for climbers of all skill levels. From beginner-friendly routes to challenging ascents, climbers can test their skills and enjoy the thrill of scaling vertical cliffs.

Zip-lining: For a unique and exhilarating experience, visitors can try zip-lining across the beautiful landscapes near Skopje. Zip-lining provides an adrenaline rush as you glide through the air, enjoying the bird's-eye view of the surroundings.

Here are some exciting adventure activities you can enjoy in Skopje (if you are on the paperback edition, go to www.getyourguide.com to book them):

1. Vodno Mountain and Matka Canyon Tour: Escape the hustle and bustle of Skopje city center and get back to nature in the Matka Canyon. Ride the cable car up Vodno Mountain, see miraculous frescoes of Byzantine art and much more. The tour lasts for about 5 hours and costs around $35.36.
2. Half Day Tour from Skopje to Matka Canyon: If you enjoy being in nature and want an experience beyond the typical tourist experience in Skopje, then this tour to Matka Canyon is perfect for you. The tour lasts for about 4 hours and costs around $31.07.
3. Matka Canyon Sightseeing Tour: Explore the stunning Matka Canyon in Macedonia on a full-day sightseeing tour from Skopje and cruise by small boat between the vertical rocks. Pass ancient houses, temples, and

medieval monasteries. The tour lasts for about 8 hours and costs around $107.14.

4. From Sofia: Skopje and Matka Canyon Day Trip: Take a day trip to Northern Macedonia and visit two of the most important sites of the country, its capital, Skopje, and the breathtaking Matka Canyon. Enjoy a walking tour through Skopje and free time in nature. The tour lasts for about 12 hours and costs around $155.36.

5. Full-Day Tour of Ohrid from Skopje: Head out from Skopje on a full-day trip to Ohrid, the top tourist destination in North Macedonia known as the Balkan Jerusalem. The tour lasts for about 10 hours and costs around $160.71.

10. Day Trips from Skopje

10.1 Matka Canyon

Located just a short distance from Skopje, Matka Canyon is a natural paradise that shouldn't be missed. This breathtaking canyon offers a serene escape from the city, with its towering cliffs, tranquil lake, and rich biodiversity. The Matka Lake, formed by the Treska River, is surrounded by steep rock formations that create a dramatic backdrop for outdoor activities.

https://www.gettyimages.com/detail/photo/canoe-on-the-matka-lake-in-matka-canyon-near-skopje-royalty-free-image/1061873284?adppopup=true

Adventure enthusiasts will find plenty to do in Matka Canyon. Explore the numerous hiking trails that wind through the canyon, offering stunning views of the surrounding landscapes and the chance to discover hidden caves and monasteries. Boat tours are available on the

97

lake, allowing you to glide through the calm waters and marvel at the untouched beauty of the canyon.

Nature lovers will appreciate the diverse flora and fauna found in Matka Canyon. The area is home to over 1,000 plant species, including rare and endemic varieties. Keep an eye out for eagles soaring above the cliffs and the elusive Balkan lynx, which is native to the region.

For those interested in history and culture, Matka Canyon is dotted with several ancient monasteries and churches. Visit the St. Andrew's Monastery, perched high on a cliff, to admire its beautiful frescoes and enjoy panoramic views of the canyon. The Church of St. Nicholas, located near the lake, is another notable religious site worth exploring.

Whether you're seeking outdoor adventure, scenic beauty, or cultural exploration, a day trip to Matka Canyon offers a memorable experience. Be sure to bring your camera to capture the stunning vistas and enjoy a picnic by the lakeside for a truly tranquil and rejuvenating day in nature.

10.2 Ohrid – UNESCO World Heritage Site:

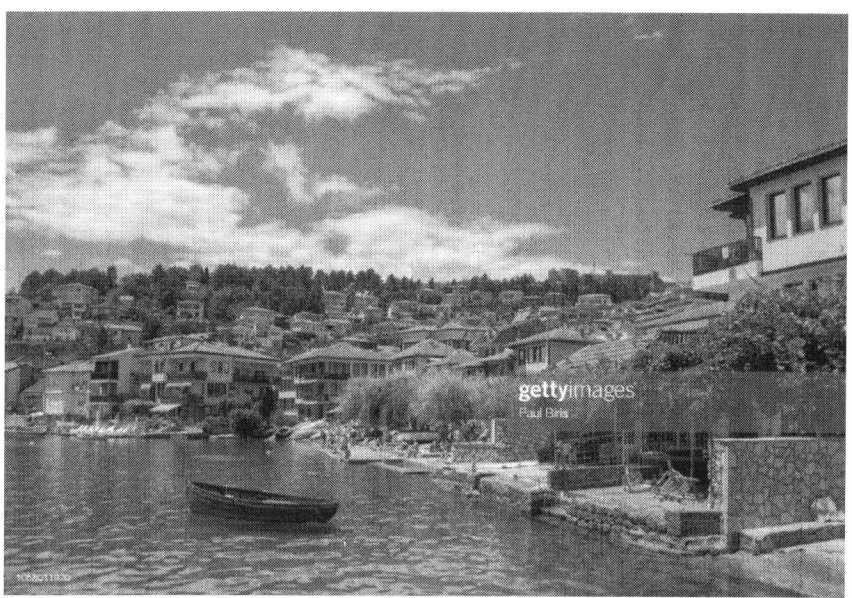

https://www.gettyimages.com/detail/photo/macedonia-ohrid-buildings-of-ohrid-old-town-royalty-free-image/1058011920?adppopup=true

Ohrid, a UNESCO World Heritage Site, is a picturesque town situated on the shores of Lake Ohrid. Known for its rich history and stunning natural beauty, Ohrid is a popular destination for visitors seeking a combination of cultural and leisure experiences.

The town of Ohrid is steeped in history, with a legacy that dates back thousands of years. Explore the narrow cobbled streets of the Old Town, where medieval churches, monasteries, and Ottoman-era buildings coexist. Visit the iconic Church of St. Sophia, which houses a remarkable collection of Byzantine frescoes. The Church of St. John at Kaneo, perched on a cliff overlooking the lake, is another must-visit attraction for its stunning architecture and panoramic views.

Lake Ohrid itself is a natural wonder and one of the oldest and deepest lakes in Europe. Take a boat ride on the crystal-clear waters and soak in the beauty of the surrounding landscapes. You can also swim, sunbathe, or simply relax on the lakeside beaches.

Nature enthusiasts will appreciate the abundance of hiking trails and nature reserves near Ohrid. Explore Galichica National Park, located between Lake Ohrid and Lake Prespa, to discover diverse ecosystems, rare plant species, and stunning vistas of the lakes and mountains.

Ohrid is also known for its lively cultural scene. Attend a performance at the Ohrid Summer Festival, which showcases a variety of music, dance, and theater events throughout the summer months. Don't miss the opportunity to sample traditional Macedonian cuisine in one of the local restaurants, where you can savor dishes like tavche gravche (baked beans), ajvar (red pepper relish), and Ohrid trout.

With its historical treasures, natural splendor, and vibrant atmosphere, Ohrid offers a captivating day trip from Skopje. Immerse yourself in its charm, explore its cultural heritage, and bask in the idyllic setting of Lake Ohrid.

10.3 Mavrovo National Park

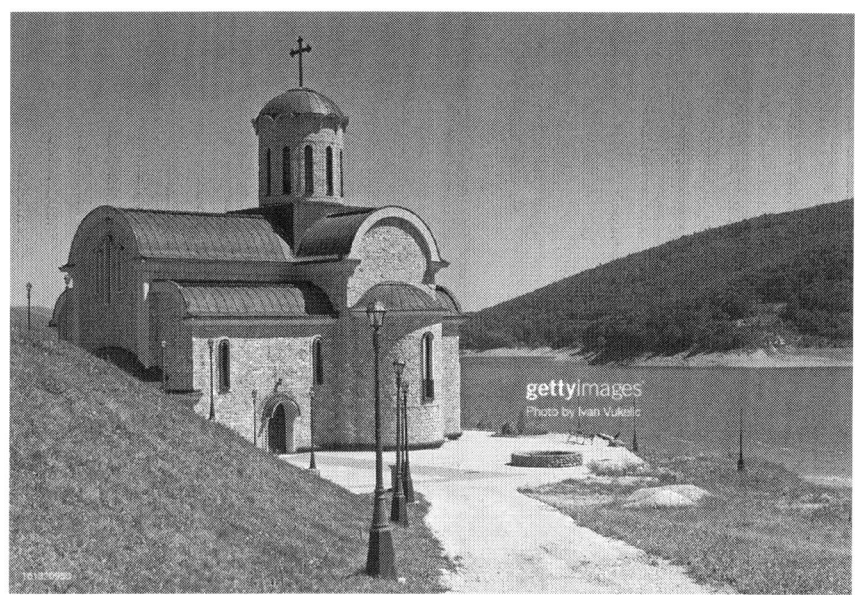

https://www.gettyimages.com/detail/photo/mavrovo-
church-royalty-free-image/161320950?adppopup=true

Mavrovo National Park is a pristine wilderness located in
the western part of North Macedonia. It is known for its
breathtaking mountain landscapes, dense forests, and
crystal-clear lakes. A day trip to Mavrovo National Park is
a treat for nature lovers and outdoor enthusiasts.

The park is dominated by the towering peaks of the Bistra
and Korab Mountains, offering opportunities for hiking,
mountaineering, and wildlife spotting. Explore the
network of hiking trails that wind through the park,
taking you to hidden valleys, serene lakes, and panoramic
viewpoints. The peak of Mount Korab, the highest peak in
North Macedonia, is a popular destination for experienced
hikers seeking a challenge and rewarding vistas.

Mavrovo National Park is also home to several picturesque lakes. The most famous among them is Lake Mavrovo, a large artificial lake created by a dam on the Mavrovska River. The tranquil waters of the lake provide a stunning backdrop for various water activities, such as boating, kayaking, and fishing.

The park boasts a rich variety of flora and fauna, with over 1,000 plant species and numerous animal species. Keep an eye out for brown bears, wolves, chamois, and various bird species as you explore the park's wilderness. Birdwatchers will be delighted by the opportunity to spot rare species such as the golden eagle and the wallcreeper.

For a touch of culture, visit the village of Mavrovo, located within the national park. Here, you can discover traditional Macedonian architecture, visit the St. Nicholas Church with its unique frescoes, and learn about the local way of life.

Mavrovo National Park is a haven for nature enthusiasts and adventurers, offering breathtaking scenery, outdoor activities, and a chance to reconnect with nature. Whether you choose to hike, swim, or simply bask in the tranquility of the surroundings, a day trip to Mavrovo National Park promises an unforgettable experience.

10.4 Bitola - The City of Consuls:

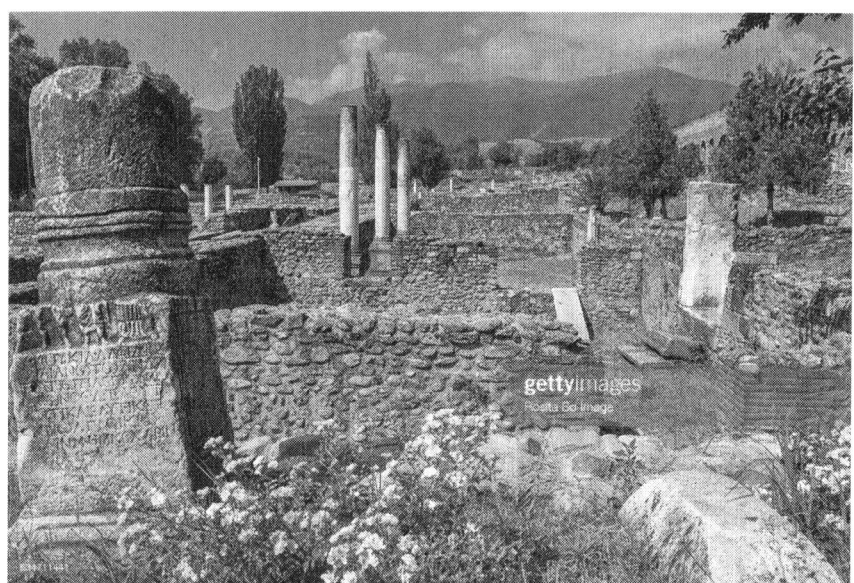

Macedonia's iconic City of Consuls is a historic city located in southwestern North Macedonia. With its well-preserved Ottoman architecture, grand boulevards, and vibrant cultural scene, Bitola offers a fascinating day trip from Skopje.

The city's history can be traced back to the ancient times, and it flourished during the Ottoman period as an important trading and cultural center. As you explore Bitola, you'll encounter numerous architectural gems, such as the Heraclea Lyncestis archaeological site, the Clock Tower, and the Yeni Mosque. The Old Bazaar is a must-visit, where you can wander through its narrow streets, browse traditional crafts, and sample local delicacies.

Bitola is also known for its cultural and artistic heritage. The city hosts the Manaki Brothers Film Festival, the oldest film festival in the Balkans, attracting filmmakers and enthusiasts from around the world. Visit the Bitola Museum to learn about the city's history and see its impressive collection of artifacts.

For a taste of the natural beauty surrounding Bitola, head to Pelister National Park. Located just a short distance from the city, the park is home to Mount Pelister, which offers excellent hiking opportunities and panoramic views. The park is known for its rare flora, including the endemic Macedonian pine, and diverse fauna, such as the Balkan chamois and brown bears.

Bitola's lively café culture adds to its charm, with numerous outdoor cafes and restaurants lining the main boulevard. Relax in one of the cafes, savoring traditional Macedonian coffee or trying local specialties like pastrmajlija (a meat pie) and tavche gravche (baked beans).

10.5 Prizren, Kosovo - Cross-border Excursion:

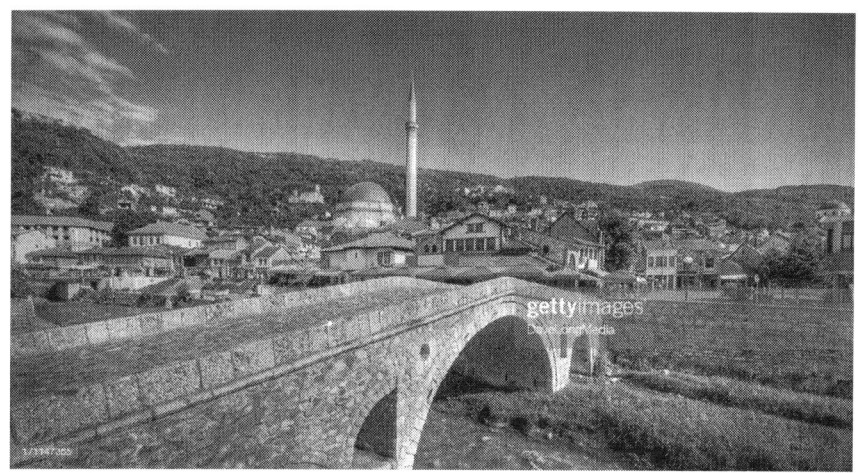

https://www.gettyimages.com/detail/photo/beautiful-view-of-ottoman-in-europe-royalty-free-image/171147365?adppopup=true

If you're interested in exploring beyond North Macedonia's borders, a day trip to Prizren in Kosovo offers a fascinating cross-cultural experience. Prizren is a historic city with a diverse heritage, characterized by its blend of Ottoman, Byzantine, and Serbian influences.

As you wander through the streets of Prizren, you'll be captivated by its well-preserved architecture, including the iconic stone bridge and the medieval fortress overlooking the city. The Sinan Pasha Mosque and the Church of Our Lady of Ljeviš are architectural marvels that reflect the city's cultural diversity.

The Shadervan Square is the heart of Prizren, bustling with activity and lined with cafes and restaurants. Take a moment to relax and soak in the vibrant atmosphere while sipping traditional Turkish tea or enjoying a flavorful Albanian meal.

The Prizren League House, a historical building dating back to the 19th century, is now a museum that showcases the city's history and cultural heritage. Explore its exhibits to gain insights into Prizren's past and its significance in the region.

Prizren is also known for its annual documentary film festival, Dokufest, which attracts filmmakers and cinephiles from around the world. If your visit aligns with the festival dates, it's an excellent opportunity to immerse yourself in the world of documentary cinema.

Located amidst stunning natural landscapes, Prizren offers opportunities for outdoor activities as well. The nearby Sharri Mountains provide a backdrop for hiking and exploring picturesque villages. Visit the Mirusha Waterfalls, a series of cascades nestled in a beautiful gorge, for a refreshing natural retreat.

A day trip to Prizren from Skopje allows you to experience the unique blend of cultures, explore historical landmarks, and appreciate the natural beauty of the region. It's an opportunity to broaden your horizons and delve into the rich tapestry of Balkan history and heritage.

10.6 Kruševo - The Highest Town in North Macedonia:

Located at an elevation of 1,350 meters (4,430 feet), Kruševo holds the title of being the highest town in North Macedonia. This charming mountain town is known for its rich history, picturesque setting, and vibrant cultural scene. Wander through the narrow cobblestone streets, lined with traditional stone houses, and admire the panoramic views of the surrounding mountains.

Kruševo is renowned for its traditional architecture and unique cultural heritage. Visit the Makedonium, a monumental structure dedicated to the Ilinden Uprising, an important event in the country's history. Explore the numerous churches and monasteries, such as the Holy Transfiguration Monastery, which dates back to the 14th century.

The town is also famous for its vibrant arts and crafts scene. Discover local artisans producing traditional ceramics, woodwork, and textiles. Don't miss the opportunity to taste Kruševo's signature dessert, called Kruševska pita, a delicious pie made with apples and walnuts.

For outdoor enthusiasts, Kruševo offers excellent hiking and paragliding opportunities. The nearby Zlato Pole and Meckin Kamen are popular hiking destinations, offering stunning views of the surrounding landscapes. If you're feeling adventurous, try paragliding from Treskavec Hill and experience the thrill of flying over the town and its scenic surroundings.

10.7 Stobi - Ancient Roman City:

Embark on a journey back in time with a day trip to Stobi, an ancient Roman city situated near the modern village of Gradsko. Once a thriving urban center, Stobi offers a fascinating glimpse into the Roman civilization that flourished in the region.

Explore the well-preserved ruins of Stobi, including the grand amphitheater, the basilicas, and the mosaics that depict intricate designs and mythological scenes. Visit the archaeological museum on-site to learn more about the history and significance of this ancient city.

Stobi is also known for its vineyards and winemaking tradition. Enjoy a wine tasting experience at one of the local wineries and savor the flavors of the region's fine wines, which have been produced for centuries.

10.8 Kokino - Ancient Megalithic Observatory:

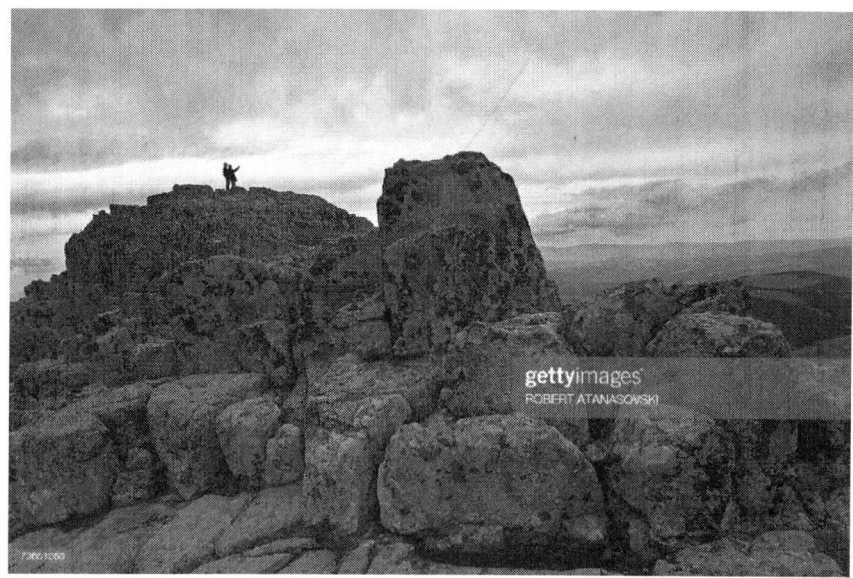

https://www.gettyimages.com/detail/news-photo/two-people-look-at-the-horizon-standing-at-the-megalithic-news-photo/73651260?adppopup=true

For those fascinated by ancient civilizations and astronomical phenomena, a day trip to Kokino is a must. Kokino is an ancient megalithic observatory located on a hilltop near the town of Kumanovo. It is believed to be one of the oldest astronomical observatories in the world.

Discover the stone markers and platforms at Kokino that were used by the ancient people to observe celestial events such as solstices and equinoxes. Marvel at the precise alignment of these structures with astronomical phenomena and learn about the advanced knowledge and skills of the ancient inhabitants.

The site also offers panoramic views of the surrounding landscapes, including the lush hills and valleys. Take a moment to absorb the peaceful ambiance and reflect on the ancient wisdom that once thrived in this mystical place.

These additional day trip options provide a diverse range of experiences, from exploring historic towns and archaeological sites to enjoying nature and uncovering ancient mysteries. Each destination offers a unique glimpse into North Macedonia's rich cultural heritage and natural beauty, providing ample opportunities for exploration and discovery.

11. Skopje 3-Day Itinerary for First Timers

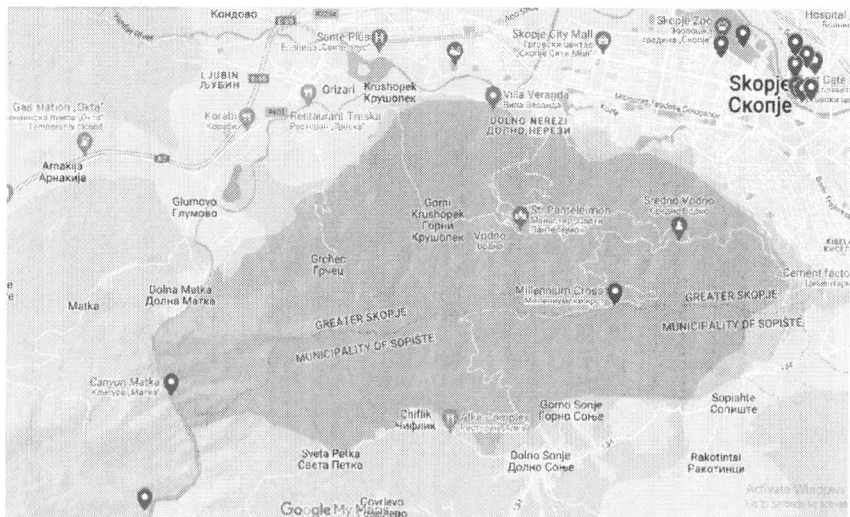

For the detailed list of destinations in this itinerary, check the Google Maps at this link:

You can also visit **bit.ly/skopjetour** or scan this QR code to get it:

Day 1 Itinerary

Morning:
Start your first day in Skopje by exploring the city's historic core. Begin with a visit to the iconic Stone Bridge, a symbol of the city, which spans the Vardar River. Take a leisurely stroll across the bridge and admire the views of the surrounding area. The bridge holds great historical significance and offers a perfect starting point to delve into Skopje's rich heritage.

Continue your walk to the Old Bazaar, one of the largest and oldest bazaars in the Balkans. Immerse yourself in the vibrant atmosphere as you wander through its narrow streets lined with shops, cafes, and traditional Ottoman-style buildings. The Old Bazaar is a treasure trove of history and culture, and you'll find a wide range of goods and souvenirs to explore. Take your time to browse through the local handicrafts, spices, and traditional Macedonian products.

As you explore the Old Bazaar, make sure to visit the Mustafa Pasha Mosque. This striking Ottoman-era mosque showcases exquisite architecture and design. Step inside to admire its beautiful interior and learn about its historical significance. Take a moment of tranquility and appreciate the peaceful atmosphere within the mosque.

Afternoon:

For lunch, head to one of the charming restaurants or cafes located in the Old Bazaar. Indulge in traditional Macedonian cuisine, which is known for its rich flavors and hearty dishes. Try some local specialties such as tavche gravche (baked beans), ajvar (a roasted red pepper relish), and kacamak (a traditional cornmeal dish).

After lunch, make your way to Skopje Fortress, also known as the Kale Fortress. This medieval fortress offers panoramic views of the city and the surrounding landscapes. Explore the fortress walls, towers, and courtyards while learning about its fascinating history. Don't forget to bring your camera, as the fortress provides fantastic photo opportunities.

Evening:

As the sun sets, head back to the city center and experience Skopje's vibrant nightlife. Start your evening at

Macedonia Square, the heart of the city, and witness the impressive fountain show that takes place every evening. Enjoy the lively atmosphere and take a moment to appreciate the grand statues and monuments that adorn the square.

For dinner, venture to **Debar Maalo,** a lively neighborhood known for its trendy restaurants and bars. This area offers a wide variety of cuisines, from traditional Macedonian to international dishes. Choose a restaurant that suits your taste and enjoy a memorable dining experience.

After dinner, explore the vibrant nightlife scene of Skopje. The city offers a range of bars, clubs, and live music venues to cater to different tastes. Dance the night away, enjoy live performances, or simply relax with a drink and soak up the energetic atmosphere.

End your first day in Skopje by taking a leisurely walk back to your accommodation, reflecting on the rich history and vibrant culture you've experienced throughout the day. Rest up and get ready for another exciting day of exploration in this captivating city.

Day 2 Itinerary

Morning:
On your second day in Skopje, venture outside the city center to explore some of its natural and cultural attractions. Start your day by visiting the Millennium Cross, one of Skopje's most iconic landmarks. Located on the summit of Mount Vodno, the Millennium Cross offers breathtaking panoramic views of the city and the surrounding landscapes. Take a cable car ride up the

mountain for a scenic journey and enjoy the stunning vistas from the top.

After taking in the views, make your way to the nearby Matka Canyon. This picturesque canyon is a paradise for nature lovers and outdoor enthusiasts. Embark on a boat tour along the emerald-green waters of the Treska River, surrounded by towering cliffs and lush vegetation. Marvel at the breathtaking rock formations and discover hidden caves, including the Vrelo Cave, one of the deepest underwater caves in the world. Enjoy the tranquility of the canyon and take advantage of the hiking trails that offer stunning viewpoints.

Afternoon:
For lunch, head back to the city center and explore the area around Macedonia Square. You'll find numerous restaurants and cafes offering a variety of cuisines. Whether you're in the mood for traditional Macedonian dishes or international flavors, there are plenty of options to satisfy your cravings.

In the afternoon, immerse yourself in Skopje's rich cultural scene by visiting its museums and art galleries. Start with the Museum of Contemporary Art, which houses a diverse collection of modern and contemporary art from Macedonia and around the world. Explore the thought-provoking exhibits and appreciate the creativity and talent on display.

Continue your cultural journey by visiting the Archaeological Museum of Macedonia. Here, you can delve into the ancient history of the region, with artifacts dating back to prehistoric times. Gain insights into the various civilizations that have shaped Macedonia throughout the ages.

Evening:
As the evening approaches, make your way to the Skopje City Park. This expansive park offers a serene escape from the bustling city streets. Take a leisurely stroll through the park's pathways, admire the lush greenery, and find a peaceful spot to relax and unwind.

For dinner, explore the lively area of Debar Maalo once again or head to the trendy district of Kapistec. Both neighborhoods offer a wide range of dining options, from cozy traditional restaurants to stylish international eateries. Indulge in delicious food and savor the flavors of Skopje's culinary scene.

After dinner, consider catching a performance at one of Skopje's theaters or concert venues. The Macedonian Opera and Ballet is a renowned institution that offers world-class performances. Check their schedule for upcoming shows and immerse yourself in the beauty of music and dance.

End your second day by enjoying a leisurely evening stroll along the banks of the Vardar River. Admire the illuminated buildings and bridges that create a magical atmosphere. Find a cozy riverside cafe or bar to relax, unwind, and reflect on the day's adventures before returning to your accommodation.

Day 3 Itinerary

Morning:
On your final day in Skopje, immerse yourself in the city's history and cultural heritage. Start your day by visiting the trendy district of Kapistec and enjoy an excellent breakfast at one of the local restaurants. Afterward, make your way to the Old Bazaar, one of the largest and oldest marketplaces in the Balkans. Stroll through its narrow, cobblestone streets and soak up the vibrant atmosphere. The bazaar is a treasure trove of shops, boutiques, and traditional craft workshops. Browse through local handicrafts, jewelry, textiles, and antiques, and find unique souvenirs to take home.

Midday:
For lunch, indulge in traditional Macedonian cuisine at one of the authentic restaurants in the Old Bazaar. Sample local specialties such as tavče gravče (a traditional bean dish), ajvar (a red pepper relish), and the famous white brined Macedonian cheese. Enjoy the warm hospitality and savor the flavors of Macedonia's culinary traditions.

From there, venture to the Skopje Aqueduct, a remarkable historical site located just outside the city center. This ancient Roman structure dates back to the 2nd century and once supplied water to the city. Marvel at the impressive arches and walk along the aqueduct to experience its grandeur up close.

Next, head to the Museum of Macedonia, located near the aqueduct. This museum offers a comprehensive overview of Macedonia's history, culture, and art. Explore its extensive collections, including archaeological artifacts, ethnographic exhibits, and artworks, and gain a deeper understanding of the country's rich heritage.

Enjoy the late afternoon in Macedonia Square, witnessing the city's transformation as the sun sets and the buildings light up. Take a moment to admire the grand statue of Alexander the Great and the iconic Fountain of Alexander.

Evening:

For your final dinner in Skopje, choose a restaurant with a view. Many rooftop restaurants in the city center offer panoramic vistas of Skopje's illuminated landmarks. Enjoy a delicious meal while taking in the breathtaking sights of the city.

After dinner, explore the city's nightlife scene. Skopje offers a vibrant nightlife with numerous bars, clubs, and live music venues. Dance the night away, enjoy live performances, or simply relax with a drink and soak up the energetic ambiance.

Before bidding farewell to Skopje, take another leisurely evening walk along the Stone Bridge. Admire the beautifully illuminated bridge, listen to the sounds of the Vardar River flowing beneath, and reflect on the memorable experiences you've had during your time in Skopje.

12. Skopje 3-Day Itinerary for Couples

https://www.gettyimages.com/detail/news-photo/bride-dances-during-a-traditional-wedding-ceremony-in-the-news-photo/1155565810?adppopup=true

Skopje features a perfect blend of history, culture, and romance. Whether you're exploring the city's ancient landmarks, strolling hand in hand through its charming streets, or indulging in its delectable cuisine, Skopje has plenty to offer for a memorable couple's getaway. This 3-day itinerary is designed to help you make the most of your time in Skopje, creating unforgettable moments and experiences together.

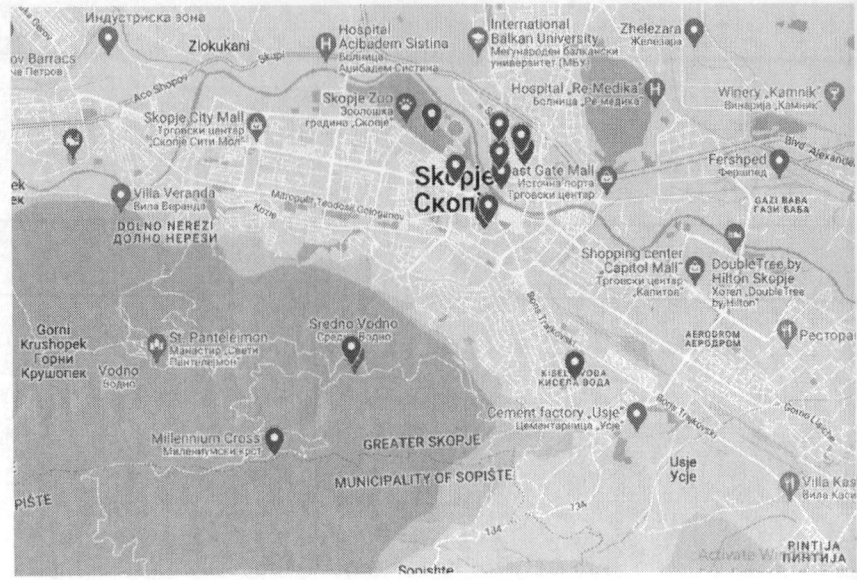

Find the Google Maps of this itinerary here:

You can also visit bit.ly/skopjeforcouples or scan this QR Code to get it:

Day 1 Itinerary

Morning:

Start your first day in Skopje with a romantic breakfast at a cozy café in the center, such as Joy or Mikel. Enjoy a cup of freshly brewed coffee and indulge in a variety of pastries and traditional Macedonian delights.

After breakfast, embark on a leisurely walk through the Old Town, known as the "Stara Čaršija." Admire the Ottoman-era architecture, explore the narrow cobblestone streets, and soak up the charming atmosphere. Discover hidden courtyards, boutique shops, and traditional craft workshops as you stroll hand in hand.

Visit the Čaršija Mosque, a stunning Ottoman mosque located in the heart of the Old Town. Take a moment to appreciate its elegant architecture and serene ambiance. If you're interested in history, consider visiting the Museum of Macedonian Struggle, which showcases artifacts and exhibits related to the country's fight for independence.

Midday:

For lunch, take a detour to Pizza Delicio in Kisela Voda. This pizzeria makes some of the best pastrmalija in the city, and the neighborhood is an underrated destination for couples. There are quite a few cute stores and unique cafes to visit, which makes the area suitable for a peaceful walk with your beloved.

Afterward, take a leisurely stroll along the Stone Bridge, one of Skopje's iconic landmarks. This beautiful bridge offers stunning views of the Vardar River and the city skyline. As you walk hand in hand, pause to admire the statues and monuments that line the bridge.

Afternoon:
In the afternoon, visit the Skopje Fortress, also known as the Kale Fortress. This ancient fortress offers panoramic views of the city and provides a serene and picturesque setting for a romantic afternoon. Explore the fortress walls, discover its towers and gates, and enjoy the peaceful ambiance of this historic site.

Next, make your way to the Millennium Cross, one of Skopje's most prominent landmarks. Take a cable car ride for two to the top of Mount Vodno, where the cross stands tall, and enjoy the breathtaking views of the city and surrounding mountains. Capture the magical moments together and create lasting memories.

Evening:
For a romantic dinner, head to one of the rooftop restaurants in the city center. These venues offer a romantic atmosphere and stunning views of Skopje's illuminated landmarks. Indulge in a candlelit dinner while savoring delicious Macedonian cuisine and fine wines.

After dinner, take a romantic evening walk along the Vardar River. The river promenade is beautifully lit up at night, creating a romantic ambiance. Hold hands as you stroll along the river, taking in the city lights and enjoying the peacefulness of the surroundings.

Day 2 Itinerary

Morning:
Start your second day in Skopje with a visit to the Museum of Contemporary Art. This impressive museum houses a collection of modern and contemporary artworks by local and international artists. Explore the various exhibits, immerse yourselves in the world of art, and engage in thought-provoking discussions about the pieces you encounter.

Afterward, take a short walk to the Memorial House of Mother Teresa, dedicated to the life and humanitarian work of the beloved Nobel laureate. Learn about Mother Teresa's inspiring journey and her selfless contributions to society. Reflect on her legacy and the values of compassion and love.

Midday:
For a romantic lunch, head to one of the charming restaurants near the Skopje City Park. Enjoy a leisurely meal surrounded by nature and greenery. Take your time to savor the flavors of Macedonian cuisine and appreciate each other's company.

After lunch, take a leisurely stroll through the Skopje City Park, a beautiful urban oasis. Find a quiet spot to sit together and enjoy the peacefulness of nature. If you're feeling adventurous, rent bicycles and explore the park's picturesque paths and trails.

Afternoon:
In the afternoon, visit the National Museum of North Macedonia, located in the city center. This museum offers a fascinating journey through the country's history and

cultural heritage. Explore its extensive collections, including archaeological artifacts, artworks, and ethnographic exhibits. Engage in conversations about history, art, and culture as you delve into the rich tapestry of North Macedonia.

Next, make your way to the Macedonian Opera and Ballet, located near the city center. Check the schedule for any performances or rehearsals taking place during your visit. If possible, attend a ballet or opera together and experience the beauty of live performances.

Evening:
For a romantic dinner, venture to the trendy Debar Maalo neighborhood. This lively area is known for its cozy restaurants and vibrant atmosphere. Explore the various dining options and choose a restaurant that suits your culinary preferences. Enjoy a romantic candlelit dinner, accompanied by live music or a cozy ambiance.

After dinner, take a romantic evening walk along the Macedonia Street, one of Skopje's bustling promenades. Explore the shops, boutiques, and cafes that line the street, and perhaps find a small memento or gift for each other.

Day 3 Itinerary

Morning:

On your final day in Skopje, escape the city and immerse yourselves in nature. Begin your day by taking a short trip to Matka Canyon, a picturesque natural gem located just outside Skopje. Embark on a boat ride along the calm waters of the canyon and admire the towering cliffs and lush vegetation. Explore the caves and enjoy the serenity of this tranquil place.

Afternoon:

Find a peaceful spot by the riverbank for a romantic picnic. Pack a basket with delicious local treats and enjoy a leisurely meal surrounded by nature's beauty. Take your time to relax, unwind, and appreciate the moments of togetherness.

After your picnic, continue your nature exploration with a hike along Vodno and the surrounding mountains. Enjoy the fresh air, the beauty of nature, and the time with your partner. Reach the summit and relish the sense of accomplishment and the breathtaking vistas that stretch before you.

For a relaxing afternoon, take a leisurely walk along the river promenade, hand in hand. Enjoy the scenery and the peacefulness of the surroundings. Find a cozy spot to sit together and watch the sunset over Skopje, creating a romantic and memorable moment.

Evening:

For your final evening in Skopje, choose a restaurant that offers a romantic atmosphere and a menu filled with exquisite culinary delights. Enjoy a candlelit dinner and toast to the wonderful experiences you've shared throughout your stay in Skopje.

After dinner, take a leisurely walk through the city center, savoring the enchanting ambiance of Skopje by night. Explore the illuminated monuments and landmarks, and perhaps stop for a nightcap at one of the trendy bars or lounges.

13. Skopje 3-Day Itinerary for Families

The city features a variety of attractions and activities that are perfect for families. From cultural sites to outdoor adventures, there's something for everyone to enjoy. This three-day itinerary will help you make the most of your family trip to Skopje, creating lasting memories and moments of joy.

Find the Google Maps of this itineraries' destinations here or visit bit.ly/SkopjeFamily

Day 1 Itinerary

Morning:
Start your first day in Skopje with a visit to the Skopje Fortress, also known as the Kale Fortress. This ancient fortress offers a glimpse into the city's history and provides stunning panoramic views of Skopje. Explore the fortress walls, climb the towers, and learn about its significance through informative displays and exhibits.

Next, head to the Old Bazaar, one of the oldest and largest bazaars in the Balkans. Stroll through its narrow streets and soak up the vibrant atmosphere. Explore the shops, boutiques, and traditional craft stores, where you can find unique souvenirs and local products.

Midday:
For lunch, stop by one of the family-friendly restaurants in the Old Bazaar. Sample delicious Macedonian dishes, such as kebabs, pita, and traditional desserts. Many restaurants in Skopje offer kid-friendly menus and accommodate dietary preferences.

After lunch, make your way to the Memorial House of Mother Teresa. This museum is dedicated to the life and work of the renowned humanitarian and Nobel laureate, Mother Teresa. Learn about her inspiring journey and the impact she had on the world. The museum features exhibits, artifacts, and multimedia presentations that will engage and educate both children and adults.

Afternoon:
In the afternoon, visit the Skopje City Park, a vast green space where families can enjoy outdoor activities. The park features playgrounds, walking paths, and recreational areas. Let your children play on the swings and slides, or have a picnic in the park while enjoying the beautiful surroundings.

Next, head to the Museum of Macedonian Struggle, located in the city center. This museum provides insight into the history of Macedonia's struggle for independence. Engage in interactive exhibits and displays that showcase the country's fight for freedom. The museum offers a unique educational experience for children, helping them understand the importance of history and national identity.

Evening:
For a memorable evening, take a leisurely walk along the Macedonia Street, Skopje's vibrant promenade. Enjoy the lively atmosphere and street performances that entertain both young and old. Stop by the fountains in the main square, where children can splash and play in the water. Grab a snack from one of the street vendors and let the whole family enjoy the festive ambiance.

Day 2 Itinerary

Morning:
Start your second day with a visit to the Skopje Zoo, a popular destination for families. This zoo is home to a diverse range of animal species from around the world. Take a leisurely stroll through the zoo and observe the animals in their natural habitats. Learn about conservation efforts and the importance of protecting wildlife.

After the zoo visit, head to the nearby Millennium Cross on Mount Vodno. Enjoy a cable car ride to the summit, offering breathtaking views of Skopje and the surrounding landscape. Take in the panoramic views and seize the moment with some beautiful family photos. At the summit, explore the area and enjoy the fresh mountain air.

Midday:

For lunch, visit one of the family-friendly restaurants near the mountain, such as Pizzeria Delicio. Satisfy the kids and try a bit of authentic Macedonian culture with some delicious pastrmalija, or head into Aerodrome to enjoy Equilibrium's blend of international and Macedonian food.

After lunch, make your way to the Skopje Aqueduct, an impressive ancient structure that once supplied water to the city. Explore the ruins and learn about its history. This site offers a great opportunity for children to learn about ancient architecture and engineering.

Afternoon:
In the afternoon, head to the Matka Canyon, located just outside Skopje. This natural wonder is perfect for a family adventure. Take a boat ride on the Matka Lake, surrounded by towering cliffs and caves. Explore the Vrelo Cave, known for its stunning stalactites and underground river. Enjoy hiking along the trails and embrace the tranquility of nature.

Evening:
For a relaxing evening, return to Skopje and visit one of the family-friendly restaurants near the city center. Choose a place with outdoor seating, where children can enjoy the lively atmosphere while parents savor traditional Macedonian cuisine.

Day 3 Itinerary

Morning:

Start your third day with a visit to the Museum of Contemporary Art, located near the city center. This museum showcases a collection of modern and contemporary artworks by local and international artists. Engage in interactive exhibits and explore various art forms, sparking creativity and imagination in children.

Next, visit the Macedonian National Theatre, an iconic cultural institution in Skopje. Check the schedule for any family-friendly performances or plays suitable for children. Enjoy a theatrical experience and witness the talents of local actors and artists.

Midday:
For lunch, choose a restaurant near the city center that offers a kid-friendly menu and a relaxed atmosphere. Enjoy a leisurely meal together, discussing the highlights of your trip and sharing your favorite moments.

Afternoon:
In the afternoon, visit the Museum of Archaeology of Macedonia, located in the heart of Skopje. This museum showcases a rich collection of archaeological artifacts that provide insight into the country's ancient history. Engage in educational exhibits and learn about the ancient civilizations that once thrived in the region. Children will have the opportunity to see ancient artifacts up close and learn about the archaeological process.

Evening:
For the final evening in Skopje, head to the city center and enjoy the vibrant nightlife. Take a walk along the Stone Bridge, illuminated by colorful lights, and soak up the festive atmosphere. Explore the bustling cafes, ice cream

shops, and souvenir stores. Consider taking a horse-drawn carriage ride for a unique experience that the whole family will enjoy.

14. Day Trip Itineraries

If one of the day trips listed earlier in the book caught
your eye but wasn't included in the three-day itineraries,
here are a series of day trip itineraries. If you want to
customize your three-day itinerary with a day trip, you
just slide any of these day trips into place to replace one of
the days in the trip. Alternatively, you can mix-and-
match with a three-day stay in Skopje and extra day trips
on the side.

Matka Canyon Itinerary

Morning:
Begin your day early with a scenic drive from Skopje to
Matka Canyon, located approximately 17 kilometers
southwest of the city. As you approach the canyon, the
landscape transforms into a picturesque natural wonder,
characterized by rugged cliffs, lush greenery, and the
tranquil blue waters of Matka Lake.

Upon arrival, take a moment to soak in the breathtaking
views of the canyon. The towering cliffs, adorned with
wildflowers and vegetation, create a stunning backdrop
against the shimmering lake. The peaceful ambiance and
untouched beauty of Matka Canyon make it a perfect
escape from the bustling city.

One of the highlights of Matka Canyon is the Church of St.
Andrew, a medieval church perched on the cliffs
overlooking the canyon. Take a leisurely hike up to the
church and explore its interior adorned with beautiful
frescoes. The church holds great historical and religious

significance, and the panoramic views from its location are simply awe-inspiring.

Mid-Morning:
After visiting the church, it's time to embark on a boat ride along Matka Lake. Board a traditional wooden boat and glide across the calm waters, immersing yourself in the tranquil atmosphere. As you sail deeper into the canyon, you'll be surrounded by the towering cliffs and the lush vegetation that lines the shores.

Keep your eyes peeled for the diverse wildlife that calls Matka Canyon home. If you're lucky, you might spot various bird species, including the majestic falcons and eagles that soar above the canyon. The boat ride offers a unique perspective of the natural beauty of Matka Canyon, allowing you to appreciate its sheer size and marvel at its geological formations.

Lunch:
After the boat ride, head to one of the local restaurants near the canyon for a delightful lunch. Indulge in traditional Macedonian cuisine and savor the flavors of regional dishes. Try local specialties such as tavche gravche (slow-cooked beans), ajvar (roasted red pepper spread), and selsko meso (village-style meat dish). Enjoy a leisurely meal while taking in the serene surroundings of the canyon.

Afternoon:
In the afternoon, continue your exploration of Matka Canyon by embarking on a hiking adventure. There are several trails to choose from, catering to different fitness levels and interests. Whether you prefer a leisurely stroll

along the lakeside or a more challenging hike up the cliffs for panoramic views, Matka Canyon has options for everyone.

One popular trail is the Vrelo Cave trail, which leads to the entrance of the deepest underwater cave in the Balkans. Explore the cave and marvel at its unique rock formations and underground streams. The cool temperature inside provides a refreshing respite from the summer heat.

Another trail worth considering is the climb to the top of Mount Shisevski, which offers panoramic views of Matka Canyon and the surrounding landscapes. The hike is moderately challenging, but the reward of breathtaking vistas makes it worthwhile.

Evening:
As the day comes to a close, take a moment to relax and soak in the tranquility of Matka Canyon. Find a peaceful spot along the shores of Matka Lake and enjoy the beauty of the setting sun casting vibrant colors across the cliffs and the water. It's a perfect opportunity to reflect on the day's adventures and appreciate the natural wonders of this hidden gem.

Finally, make your way back to Skopje, taking with you memories of the stunning landscapes, the cultural heritage, and the peaceful ambiance of Matka Canyon. The day trip to Matka Canyon promises an unforgettable experience for nature enthusiasts, history buffs, and anyone seeking a peaceful escape into the heart of North Macedonia's natural beauty.

Mavrovo National Park Day Trip Itinerary

If you're looking to immerse yourself in the beauty of nature, a day trip to Mavrovo National Park is a perfect choice. Located about 70 kilometers west of Skopje, this national park is known for its stunning landscapes, pristine lakes, and abundant wildlife. Here's a suggested itinerary to make the most of your day in Mavrovo National Park:

Morning: Departure from Skopje to Mavrovo National Park

Start your day early to make the most of your time in Mavrovo National Park. After breakfast, hop in a car or hire a driver to take you on the approximately 1.5 to 2-hour journey from Skopje to the national park. The drive itself is quite scenic, taking you through picturesque countryside and offering glimpses of the rugged mountain ranges that surround the park.

Mid-Morning: Exploring the Natural Wonders of Mavrovo National Park

Upon arrival at Mavrovo National Park, take a moment to soak in the serene atmosphere and marvel at the panoramic views of the surrounding mountains. The park is characterized by its diverse landscapes, including dense forests, alpine meadows, and crystal-clear lakes.

One of the highlights of the park is Lake Mavrovo, a large reservoir surrounded by mountains. Enjoy a leisurely stroll along the lake's shoreline, take in the fresh mountain air, and capture some memorable photos of the scenic surroundings.

For nature enthusiasts, Mavrovo National Park offers numerous hiking trails that cater to different fitness levels. Consider embarking on a hike to explore the park's hidden gems, such as the charming village of Galichnik or the impressive cliffs of Mount Bistra. If you prefer a more relaxed experience, opt for a boat ride on Lake Mavrovo or simply find a peaceful spot to sit and enjoy the tranquility of nature.

Afternoon: Indulge in Local Cuisine and Cultural Delights

After a morning of exploration, satisfy your hunger with a delicious meal at one of the local restaurants or cafes in the area. Mavrovo is known for its traditional Macedonian cuisine, so be sure to try some regional specialties like tavche gravche (baked beans), pastrmajlija (a type of flatbread with toppings), or koriditse (grilled meat skewers). Pair your meal with a glass of local wine or rakija (fruit brandy) for a complete culinary experience.

After lunch, take the opportunity to delve into the cultural side of Mavrovo National Park. Visit the nearby village of Galichnik, known for its traditional architecture and vibrant folklore. Explore the cobblestone streets, admire the stone houses with their distinctive red roofs, and perhaps even catch a local festival or celebration if timing permits.

Evening: Return to Skopje with Lasting Memories

As the day comes to a close, reflect on the beautiful moments and experiences you've had in Mavrovo National Park. Depart from the park in the late afternoon, enjoying the scenic drive back to Skopje. Take in the changing landscapes as the sun sets behind the mountains, casting a warm glow over the countryside.

Arrive back in Skopje in the evening, feeling rejuvenated and filled with memories of your day in Mavrovo National Park. Take the opportunity to relax and unwind, or if you still have some energy, explore the vibrant city's nightlife and culinary scene.

Ohrid Day Trip Itinerary

You can make a short visit to Lake Ohrid as part of your Mavrovo National Park day trip, but the area is rich with natural beauty and architecture to the point you can easily spend a whole day here.

Morning:
Begin your day early by embarking on a scenic three-hour drive from Skopje to the enchanting city of Ohrid, nestled on the shores of Lake Ohrid. As you journey through picturesque landscapes, passing rural villages, rolling hills, and glimpses of the majestic lake, you'll be captivated by the natural beauty of the region.

Upon arrival in Ohrid, make your way to the mesmerizing old town, a UNESCO World Heritage Site renowned for its rich history and stunning architecture. Start your exploration at the iconic Ohrid Castle, perched atop a hill with panoramic views of the city, the lake, and the surrounding mountains. Explore the ancient fortress

138

walls, step inside the medieval museum, and immerse yourself in the historical ambiance.

Mid-Morning:
Descend from the castle and meander through the narrow cobblestone streets of the old town. Admire the charming traditional houses, quaint shops, and inviting cafes that line the streets. As you stroll, make your way to the Church of St. Sophia, a magnificent Byzantine masterpiece adorned with intricate frescoes depicting biblical scenes and saints. Marvel at the artistry and absorb the spiritual atmosphere within its ancient walls.

Continue your journey to the Church of St. John at Kaneo, a picturesque and iconic landmark perched on a cliff overlooking Lake Ohrid. This 13th-century Orthodox church boasts breathtaking views of the azure waters and surrounding mountains. Step inside and admire the interior adorned with colorful frescoes that narrate religious stories. Take a moment to soak in the tranquil ambiance of this spiritual haven.

Lunch:
Take a break from your exploration and indulge in a delightful lunch at one of the local restaurants in the old town. Treat your taste buds to the flavors of traditional Macedonian cuisine, which often includes fresh fish from Lake Ohrid, grilled meats, and an array of savory and hearty dishes. Savor the regional specialties, accompanied by a glass of local wine, and immerse yourself in the culinary delights of the area.

Afternoon:

In the afternoon, continue your exploration along the lakeside promenade, which stretches along the tranquil shores of Lake Ohrid. Take in the mesmerizing vistas of the crystal-clear waters and the distant mountains, and let the serene atmosphere envelop you. You may choose to relax on one of the lakeside benches, savoring the tranquility, or opt for a leisurely stroll along the promenade, appreciating the idyllic setting.

For a truly enriching experience, make your way to the Ancient Theatre, a well-preserved amphitheater from the Hellenistic period. Marvel at the grandeur of this archaeological gem, with its tiered seating and commanding stage. Imagine the performances that once took place in this historic venue, and soak in the ambiance of ancient times.

Next, head to the **Bay of Bones Museum**, an intriguing archaeological site located on Lake Ohrid's shoreline. This unique museum offers a glimpse into prehistoric life with its reconstructed pile-dwelling settlement. Explore the wooden walkways that lead to the museum's platforms, where you can admire the preserved remains of ancient dwellings and learn about the region's fascinating history.

Evening:
As the sun begins its descent, make your way back to the old town to witness the magical sunset over Lake Ohrid. Find a serene spot along the shoreline or a cozy cafe with a lake view to soak in the breathtaking panorama. As the sky transforms into hues of orange and purple, creating a mesmerizing spectacle, let the beauty of the moment leave an indelible mark on your memory.

Before bidding farewell to Ohrid, take the opportunity to explore the vibrant bazaar. Wander through the bustling market stalls, offering a treasure trove of local crafts, handmade souvenirs, and unique keepsakes. Choose a memento to remind you of your visit to this enchanting city and support the local artisans.

Day Trip to Bitola - The City of Consuls

Bitola, often referred to as "The City of Consuls," is a charming destination located approximately 175 kilometers south of Skopje. Known for its rich history, architectural heritage, and vibrant cultural scene, Bitola offers a fascinating glimpse into the past. Here's a suggested itinerary for a day trip to Bitola:

Morning: Departure from Skopje to Bitola

Start your day early to make the most of your time in Bitola. After breakfast, embark on a scenic journey from Skopje to Bitola, which takes around 2.5 to 3 hours by car. As you leave Skopje behind, the landscapes gradually change, showcasing the beauty of North Macedonia's southern region.

Mid-Morning: Exploring Bitola's Historical and Cultural Sites

Upon arrival in Bitola, begin your exploration of this historic city. Start with a visit to Shirok Sokak, Bitola's vibrant pedestrian street lined with cafes, restaurants, and shops. Take a leisurely stroll along the cobblestone street, soak in the lively atmosphere, and perhaps enjoy a coffee or traditional snack at one of the local establishments.

From Shirok Sokak, head to the Bitola Clock Tower, an iconic landmark that offers panoramic views of the city and its surroundings. Climb to the top for a bird's-eye perspective and capture some memorable photos.

Next, make your way to the magnificent Heraclea Lyncestis, an ancient city that dates back to the 4th century BC. Explore the well-preserved ruins, including the theater, Roman baths, and various mosaics that provide insights into the city's past. The onsite museum displays artifacts unearthed during archaeological excavations, further enhancing the historical experience.

Afternoon: Immersion in Bitola's Cultural Scene

As lunchtime approaches, venture into one of Bitola's local restaurants or taverns to savor traditional Macedonian cuisine. Treat your taste buds to dishes like tavche gravche (baked beans), ajvar (roasted red pepper spread), or kebapi (grilled meat). Pair your meal with a glass of Macedonian wine or rakija for an authentic culinary experience.

After lunch, continue your cultural exploration by visiting the Church of St. Demetrius, an exquisite Orthodox church adorned with beautiful frescoes and icons. Take a moment to appreciate the intricate details and serene ambiance of this religious site.

Another notable stop in Bitola is the Church of St. John at Kaneo, situated on a hill overlooking Lake Ohrid. Marvel at the stunning panoramic views of the lake and its surroundings, and explore the church's interior, adorned with religious artwork and frescoes.

Lastly, visit the Ancient Theatre, a well-preserved amphitheater that once hosted theatrical performances during the Roman era. Take a seat in the stone seats and imagine the grand spectacles that took place in this historic venue.

Evening: Return to Skopje with Lasting Memories

As the day draws to a close, begin your journey back to Skopje, reflecting on the wonderful experiences you've had in Bitola. Enjoy the scenic drive through the countryside, savoring the landscapes and contemplating the historical significance of the places you've visited.

Arrive back in Skopje in the evening, feeling enriched by the cultural immersion and historical discoveries of Bitola. Take some time to relax and unwind, perhaps enjoying a leisurely dinner at one of Skopje's restaurants or exploring the city's vibrant nightlife.

Prizren, Kosovo Day Trip Itinerary

Prizren, located in neighboring Kosovo, is a picturesque town that offers a unique blend of cultures and history. Known for its well-preserved Ottoman architecture, cobblestone streets, and vibrant atmosphere, Prizren is an excellent destination for a day trip from Skopje. Here's a suggested itinerary for exploring Prizren:

Morning: Departure from Skopje to Prizren

Start your day early to make the most of your time in Prizren. After breakfast, embark on a scenic journey from Skopje to Prizren. The drive takes approximately 2.5 to 3 hours, crossing the border between North Macedonia and Kosovo. Be sure to have your passport or identification documents ready for border control.

Mid-Morning: Exploring Prizren's Old Town

Upon arrival in Prizren, head straight to the Old Town area, which is the heart and soul of the city. Begin your exploration at Shadervan Square, a charming square with a beautiful Ottoman-style fountain. Take a moment to admire the architecture and soak in the ambiance of the historic surroundings.

From Shadervan Square, wander through the narrow streets lined with colorful houses, shops, and cafes. Explore the numerous mosques, churches, and historical buildings that showcase Prizren's multicultural heritage. Don't miss a visit to the impressive Sinan Pasha Mosque, a magnificent Ottoman mosque known for its elegant architecture and ornate interior.

Continue your stroll to the medieval fortress of Prizren, known as Kalaja. Climb to the top of the fortress walls for panoramic views of the city and the surrounding landscape. Take your time to explore the fortress grounds, discovering ancient ruins and enjoying the serene atmosphere.

Afternoon: Culinary Delights and Cultural Experiences

As lunchtime approaches, indulge in the diverse culinary offerings of Prizren. The town is renowned for its delicious traditional cuisine, so be sure to try local specialties such as mantia (dumplings), tavë kosi (yogurt-based casserole), and baklava (sweet pastry). There are plenty of restaurants and cafes in the Old Town where you can savor these culinary delights.

After lunch, immerse yourself in Prizren's cultural scene by visiting the League of Prizren Museum. This museum provides insights into the historic League of Prizren, a political organization that played a significant role in the preservation of Albanian identity during the Ottoman Empire. Explore the exhibits, artifacts, and multimedia presentations that highlight the city's cultural heritage.

Next, make your way to the Church of Our Lady of Ljeviš, a UNESCO World Heritage site. This medieval Serbian Orthodox church is renowned for its stunning architecture and intricate frescoes. Take your time to admire the exquisite artwork and learn about the historical and cultural significance of the church.

Evening

As the day comes to an end, begin your journey back to Skopje, reflecting on the enchanting experiences and cultural encounters you've had in Prizren. Enjoy the scenic drive through the picturesque landscapes, savoring the memories of the town's rich history and vibrant atmosphere.

Day Trip to Kruševo - The Highest Town in North Macedonia

Nestled high in the mountains of North Macedonia, Kruševo is a charming town known for its rich history, stunning vistas, and unique cultural heritage. As the highest town in the country, Kruševo offers a refreshing escape from the bustling city life. Here's a suggested itinerary for a day trip to Kruševo:

Morning: Departure from Skopje to Kruševo

Start your day early and embark on a scenic drive from Skopje to Kruševo. The journey takes approximately 2.5 to 3 hours, winding through picturesque mountain roads. Enjoy the breathtaking views of the surrounding landscapes as you make your way to the highest town in North Macedonia.

Mid-Morning: Exploring Kruševo's Historic Center

Upon arrival in Kruševo, make your way to the town's historic center, known for its well-preserved traditional architecture and narrow cobblestone streets. Begin your exploration at Makedonium, a grand monument dedicated to the Ilinden Uprising and a symbol of the town's rich history. Climb to the top of the monument for panoramic views of Kruševo and the surrounding mountains.

From Makedonium, stroll through the charming streets of the old town, admiring the traditional stone houses and quaint cafes. Discover the unique character of Kruševo as you explore its historical sites, including the Mečkin

Kamen (Bear Stone) monument and the Church of St. Nikola, famous for its beautiful iconostasis.

Midday: Cultural Experiences and Local Cuisine

As lunchtime approaches, immerse yourself in Kruševo's cultural scene and culinary delights. Visit the Kruševo Museum, housed in a beautifully restored 19th-century house, to learn more about the town's history, culture, and art. The museum exhibits a collection of artifacts, traditional costumes, and artwork that showcase Kruševo's rich heritage.

Afterward, treat yourself to a delicious meal at one of the local restaurants, savoring traditional Macedonian cuisine. Try local specialties such as tavče gravče (baked beans), ajvar (red pepper relish), and pastrmajlija (a traditional meat pie). Enjoy the warm hospitality of the locals as you indulge in these mouthwatering flavors.

Afternoon: Nature Walks and Scenic Views

After lunch, venture into the natural beauty surrounding Kruševo. Take a leisurely walk along the Kruševo Ring, a scenic trail that encircles the town and offers breathtaking panoramic views of the mountains and valleys. Enjoy the fresh mountain air and immerse yourself in the tranquility of the surroundings.

For those seeking more adventure, hike up to Meckin Kamen, a prominent peak overlooking Kruševo. The hike takes approximately 1.5 hours and rewards you with stunning vistas of the town and the surrounding landscapes. Take your time to soak in the beauty of the scenery and capture memorable photographs.

Evening: Return to Skopje with Lasting Memories

As the day comes to an end, start your journey back to Skopje, cherishing the memories of your day trip to Kruševo. Reflect on the unique cultural experiences, the stunning views, and the warm hospitality you encountered in this mountain town.

Arrive back in Skopje in the evening, feeling rejuvenated and inspired by the beauty of Kruševo. Take some time to relax and reflect on the day's adventures, perhaps enjoying a leisurely dinner at a local restaurant or exploring Skopje's vibrant nightlife. Carry the memories of Kruševo with you as you continue your journey through North Macedonia.

Note: This itinerary is a suggested guide for a day trip to Kruševo. Feel free to customize it according to your preferences and interests. Consider the weather conditions and be prepared with comfortable walking shoes, appropriate clothing layers, and a camera to capture the stunning scenery.

Stobi Day Trip Itinerary

Step back in time and explore the fascinating ruins of Stobi, an ancient Roman city located in central North Macedonia. This day trip will take you on a journey through history, uncovering the remnants of an ancient civilization. Here's a suggested itinerary for a day trip to Stobi:

Morning: Departure from Skopje to Stobi

Start your day early with a comfortable drive from Skopje to Stobi, which takes approximately 1.5 to 2 hours. Enjoy the scenic route as you make your way to the archaeological site of Stobi, located near the Vardar River.

Mid-Morning: Exploring the Ruins of Stobi

Upon arrival at Stobi, prepare to be amazed by the well-preserved ruins that tell the story of the ancient city. Begin your exploration at the entrance gate, where you can see the remains of the city walls and the impressive columns that once adorned the main streets.

As you wander through the site, discover the ancient structures that once thrived here. Visit the Stobi Theater, an impressive amphitheater that once hosted theatrical performances and gatherings. Marvel at the intricate mosaic floors of the ancient houses and villas, which provide a glimpse into the daily life of the people who lived in Stobi.

Don't miss the opportunity to explore the early Christian basilicas, such as the grand Episcopal Basilica, which features beautiful frescoes and intricate architectural details. Learn about the religious significance of these sites and imagine the vibrant community that once existed within the walls of Stobi.

Midday: Cultural Insights and Local Flavors

After immersing yourself in the ancient history of Stobi, take a break for lunch and enjoy some local cuisine. There are several restaurants and cafes near the archaeological site where you can savor traditional Macedonian dishes. Indulge in local specialties like kebapi (grilled meat), shopska salad (fresh vegetable salad with feta cheese), and traditional desserts.

While enjoying your meal, take in the peaceful ambiance of the surrounding countryside, dotted with vineyards and rolling hills. North Macedonia is known for its wine production, so be sure to try some of the region's finest wines, which pair perfectly with the local cuisine.

Afternoon: Discovering the Nearby Attractions

In the afternoon, continue your exploration by visiting some nearby attractions that complement your day trip to Stobi. One recommended stop is the Church of St. John at Kaneo, located on the shores of Lake Ohrid. This iconic church offers breathtaking views of the lake and the surrounding mountains. Take your time to admire the Byzantine architecture and soak in the tranquil atmosphere.

Next, head to the Ancient Theatre of Ohrid, another significant historical site. Marvel at the well-preserved theater, which dates back to the Hellenistic period. Imagine the performances that took place on this stage and appreciate the architectural marvel of the ancient Greeks.

To conclude your day trip, visit the Bay of Bones Museum, situated on Lake Ohrid. This unique museum showcases a reconstruction of an ancient prehistoric settlement built on stilts. Explore the exhibition halls to learn about the history of the region and the ancient civilizations that thrived on the shores of Lake Ohrid.

Evening: Return to Skopje with Lasting Memories

As the day comes to an end, start your journey back to Skopje, reminiscing about the wonders of Stobi and the surrounding attractions. Reflect on the rich history and cultural heritage you experienced throughout the day.

Arrive back in Skopje in the evening, filled with memories of the ancient Roman city of Stobi, the stunning views of Lake Ohrid, and the intriguing insights into North Macedonia's past. Take some time to relax and enjoy a leisurely dinner in Skopje, savoring the flavors and reflecting on the highlights of your day trip.

This concludes the suggested itinerary for a day trip to Stobi. Feel free to modify the itinerary based on your preferences and available time. Remember to check the opening hours of the sites and plan your visit accordingly. Enjoy your exploration of Stobi and the surrounding attractions, immersing yourself in the rich history and captivating beauty of North Macedonia.

Kokino Day Trip Itinerary

Embark on a fascinating journey to Kokino, an ancient megalithic observatory located in the northeastern part of Macedonia. This day trip will take you to one of the oldest astronomical observatories in the world, where you can witness the remnants of an ancient civilization's astronomical practices. Here's a suggested itinerary for a day trip to Kokino:

Morning: Departure from Skopje to Kokino

Start your day early with a scenic drive from Skopje to Kokino, which takes approximately 2 to 2.5 hours. As you make your way through the picturesque landscapes, enjoy the beauty of the countryside and the anticipation of the ancient site that awaits you.

Mid-Morning: Exploring the Megalithic Observatory

Upon arrival at Kokino, prepare to be astounded by the ancient observatory that dates back over 3,800 years. Begin your exploration at the visitor center, where you can gather information about the site and its significance. Engage with the knowledgeable staff who can provide insights into the astronomical knowledge and practices of the ancient civilization that once inhabited this area.

As you venture further into the site, marvel at the impressive stone circles, platforms, and markers that were used to observe celestial events. These megalithic structures were carefully aligned with the positions of the sun, moon, and stars, showcasing the advanced astronomical knowledge of the ancient people who inhabited Kokino.

Take your time to appreciate the panoramic views from the observatory. The elevated location offers breathtaking vistas of the surrounding landscape, enhancing the sense of wonder and connection to the ancient world.

Midday: Cultural Insights and Local Delights

After immersing yourself in the wonders of Kokino, take a break for a delightful lunch. While there are no restaurants within the immediate vicinity, you can pack a picnic lunch to enjoy amidst the natural beauty that surrounds the observatory. Find a peaceful spot, set up a blanket, and savor a delicious meal while soaking in the serene atmosphere.

During your lunch break, take the opportunity to reflect on the fascinating history of Kokino and its significance as an ancient megalithic observatory. Appreciate the ingenuity and knowledge of the ancient civilization that left behind such remarkable structures.

Afternoon: Exploring the Surrounding Area

In the afternoon, continue your exploration by visiting some nearby attractions that complement your day trip to Kokino. One notable stop is the Church of St. John the Baptist in Kratovo, a charming town known for its well-preserved architecture and rich history. Admire the beautiful frescoes and architectural details of the church, which dates back to the 14th century.

Next, consider visiting the Stone Dolls of Kuklica, an intriguing natural phenomenon located near Kratovo. These stone formations, resembling human figures, were created over thousands of years through natural erosion processes. Explore the area and marvel at the unique rock formations that stand as a testament to the forces of nature.

Evening: Return to Skopje with Lasting Memories

As the day comes to a close, begin your return journey to Skopje, cherishing the memories of your visit to Kokino and the surrounding attractions. Reflect on the ancient wisdom and astronomical knowledge that you've encountered throughout the day.

Arrive back in Skopje in the evening, with a sense of awe and appreciation for the ancient observatory of Kokino and the cultural treasures of Kratovo and Kuklica. Take some time to relax, savor a delicious dinner, and share your experiences with fellow travelers or loved ones.

Kruševo Day Trip Itinerary

Nestled high in the mountains of North Macedonia, Kruševo is a charming town known for its rich history, stunning vistas, and unique cultural heritage. As the highest town in the country, Kruševo offers a refreshing escape from the bustling city life. Here's a suggested itinerary for a day trip to Kruševo:

Morning: Departure from Skopje to Kruševo

Start your day early and embark on a scenic drive from Skopje to Kruševo. The journey takes approximately 2.5 to 3 hours, winding through picturesque mountain roads. Enjoy the breathtaking views of the surrounding landscapes as you make your way to the highest town in North Macedonia.

Mid-Morning: Exploring Kruševo's Historic Center

Upon arrival in Kruševo, make your way to the town's historic center, known for its well-preserved traditional architecture and narrow cobblestone streets. Begin your exploration at Makedonium, a grand monument dedicated to the Ilinden Uprising and a symbol of the town's rich history. Climb to the top of the monument for panoramic views of Kruševo and the surrounding mountains.

From Makedonium, stroll through the charming streets of the old town, admiring the traditional stone houses and quaint cafes. Discover the unique character of Kruševo as you explore its historical sites, including the Mečkin Kamen (Bear Stone) monument and the Church of St. Nikola, famous for its beautiful iconostasis.

Midday: Cultural Experiences and Local Cuisine

As lunchtime approaches, immerse yourself in Kruševo's cultural scene and culinary delights. Visit the Kruševo Museum, housed in a beautifully restored 19th-century house, to learn more about the town's history, culture, and art. The museum exhibits a collection of artifacts, traditional costumes, and artwork that showcase Kruševo's rich heritage.

Afterward, treat yourself to a delicious meal at one of the local restaurants, savoring traditional Macedonian cuisine. Try local specialties such as tavče gravče (baked beans), ajvar (red pepper relish), and pastrmajlija (a traditional meat pie). Enjoy the warm hospitality of the locals as you indulge in these mouthwatering flavors.

Afternoon: Nature Walks and Scenic Views

After lunch, venture into the natural beauty surrounding Kruševo. Take a leisurely walk along the Kruševo Ring, a scenic trail that encircles the town and offers breathtaking panoramic views of the mountains and valleys. Enjoy the fresh mountain air and immerse yourself in the tranquility of the surroundings.

For those seeking more adventure, hike up to Meckin Kamen, a prominent peak overlooking Kruševo. The hike takes approximately 1.5 hours and rewards you with stunning vistas of the town and the surrounding landscapes. Take your time to soak in the beauty of the scenery and capture memorable photographs.

Evening: Return to Skopje with Lasting Memories

As the day comes to an end, start your journey back to Skopje, cherishing the memories of your day trip to Kruševo. Reflect on the unique cultural experiences, the stunning views, and the warm hospitality you encountered in this mountain town.

Arrive back in Skopje in the evening, feeling rejuvenated and inspired by the beauty of Kruševo. Take some time to relax and reflect on the day's adventures, perhaps enjoying a leisurely dinner at a local restaurant or exploring Skopje's vibrant nightlife. Carry the memories of Kruševo with you as you continue your journey through North Macedonia.

Note: This itinerary is a suggested guide for a day trip to Kruševo. Feel free to customize it according to your preferences and interests. Consider the weather conditions and be prepared with comfortable walking shoes, appropriate clothing layers, and a camera to capture the stunning scenery.

Bitola Day Trip Itinerary

Bitola, often referred to as "The City of Consuls," is a charming destination located approximately 175 kilometers south of Skopje. Known for its rich history, architectural heritage, and vibrant cultural scene, Bitola offers a fascinating glimpse into the past. Here's a suggested itinerary for a day trip to Bitola:

Morning: Departure from Skopje to Bitola

Start your day early to make the most of your time in Bitola. After breakfast, embark on a scenic journey from Skopje to Bitola, which takes around 2.5 to 3 hours by car. As you leave Skopje behind, the landscapes gradually change, showcasing the beauty of North Macedonia's southern region.

Mid-Morning: Exploring Bitola's Historical and Cultural Sites

Upon arrival in Bitola, begin your exploration of this historic city. Start with a visit to Shirok Sokak, Bitola's vibrant pedestrian street lined with cafes, restaurants, and shops. Take a leisurely stroll along the cobblestone street, soak in the lively atmosphere, and perhaps enjoy a coffee or traditional snack at one of the local establishments.

From Shirok Sokak, head to the Bitola Clock Tower, an iconic landmark that offers panoramic views of the city and its surroundings. Climb to the top for a bird's-eye perspective and capture some memorable photos.

Next, make your way to the magnificent Heraclea Lyncestis, an ancient city that dates back to the 4th century BC. Explore the well-preserved ruins, including the theater, Roman baths, and various mosaics that provide insights into the city's past. The onsite museum displays artifacts unearthed during archaeological excavations, further enhancing the historical experience.

Afternoon: Immersion in Bitola's Cultural Scene

As lunchtime approaches, venture into one of Bitola's local restaurants or taverns to savor traditional Macedonian cuisine. Treat your taste buds to dishes like tavche gravche (baked beans), ajvar (roasted red pepper spread), or kebapi (grilled meat). Pair your meal with a glass of Macedonian wine or rakija for an authentic culinary experience.

After lunch, continue your cultural exploration by visiting the Church of St. Demetrius, an exquisite Orthodox church adorned with beautiful frescoes and icons. Take a moment to appreciate the intricate details and serene ambiance of this religious site.

Another notable stop in Bitola is the Church of St. John at Kaneo, situated on a hill overlooking Lake Ohrid. Marvel at the stunning panoramic views of the lake and its surroundings, and explore the church's interior, adorned with religious artwork and frescoes.

Lastly, visit the Ancient Theatre, a well-preserved amphitheater that once hosted theatrical performances during the Roman era. Take a seat in the stone seats and imagine the grand spectacles that took place in this historic venue.

Evening: Return to Skopje with Lasting Memories

As the day draws to a close, begin your journey back to Skopje, reflecting on the wonderful experiences you've had in Bitola. Enjoy the scenic drive through the countryside, savoring the landscapes and contemplating the historical significance of the places you've visited.

Arrive back in Skopje in the evening, feeling enriched by the cultural immersion and historical discoveries of Bitola. Take some time to relax and unwind, perhaps enjoying a leisurely dinner at one of Skopje's restaurants or exploring the city's vibrant nightlife.

15. Practical Information and Tips

15.1 Currency and Money

When visiting Skopje, it's essential to have an understanding of the local currency and money matters to ensure a smooth and hassle-free experience. The official currency in North Macedonia is the Macedonian Denar (MKD). Here are some key points to know about currency and money:

Currency Exchange: The most convenient place to exchange currency is at banks and authorized exchange offices. These can be found throughout Skopje, including at the airport and in popular tourist areas. It's advisable to compare exchange rates and fees to get the best value for your money.

ATMs: Skopje has a widespread network of ATMs, which accept major international debit and credit cards. They can be found in banks, shopping centers, and other convenient locations. Keep in mind that some smaller establishments may only accept cash, so it's always wise to carry some local currency.

Credit Cards: Credit cards are widely accepted in larger hotels, restaurants, and stores in Skopje. However, it's a good idea to carry some cash, especially for smaller establishments, local markets, and transportation services.

Tipping: Tipping in Skopje is not mandatory, but it's appreciated for good service. As a general guideline, a tip of around 10% of the total bill is customary in restaurants.

Tipping taxi drivers and hotel staff is also common, usually rounding up the fare or leaving a small amount as a gesture of appreciation.

15.2 Tipping and Gratuity

Tipping practices in Skopje may vary slightly from other countries, so it's helpful to be familiar with local customs to ensure appropriate gratuity. In general, tipping is seen as an option and not required. However, typical tipping habits in Macedonia are as follows:

Restaurants: In Skopje, it is customary to leave a tip of around 10% of the total bill at restaurants if you are satisfied with the service. Some restaurants may include a service charge on the bill, so be sure to check before adding an additional tip. If the service charge is included, leaving a small amount as a token of appreciation is still welcomed.

Cafes and Bars: Tipping in cafes and bars is not as common as in restaurants, but it's always appreciated if you receive exceptional service. You can round up the bill or leave a small amount as a gesture of appreciation.

Hotels: It's customary to tip hotel staff, particularly the bellhop or porter who assists with your luggage. A small tip of around 50 to 100 MKD per bag is appropriate. If you receive exceptional service from the hotel staff, you can consider leaving a tip at the end of your stay.

Taxi Drivers: Tipping taxi drivers in Skopje is not mandatory, but rounding up the fare or leaving a small amount as a gesture of appreciation is common practice. If the driver provides exceptional service or goes above and beyond, you may choose to tip a bit more.

15.3 Electricity and Adapters

When traveling to Skopje, it's important to know about the electricity standards and whether you need an adapter for your electronic devices. Here are some key details:

Voltage: The standard voltage in Skopje is 220-240 volts. If your electrical devices are not compatible with this voltage range, you will need a voltage converter.

Plug Types: Skopje uses the European-style plug, known as Type C or Type F. The plugs have two round pins. If your devices have a different plug type, you will need a travel adapter to plug them into the outlets.

Adapters and Converters: It's recommended to bring a universal travel adapter that can accommodate various plug types. This way, you can use it not only in Skopje but also in other countries that may have different plug standards. If your devices require a different voltage, you will also need a voltage converter.

Availability of Adapters: Travel adapters can be found in most electronic stores and travel supply shops. It's advisable to purchase an adapter before your trip to ensure you have the necessary equipment upon arrival in Skopje.

15.4 Internet and Wi-Fi Access

Staying connected to the internet is essential for many travelers, whether for communication, navigation, or accessing travel information. Skopje offers various options for internet and Wi-Fi access. Here's what you need to know:

Wi-Fi in Accommodations: Most hotels, guesthouses, and hostels in Skopje provide complimentary Wi-Fi access for their guests. The quality and speed of the connection may vary, so it's advisable to check with your accommodation beforehand.

Public Wi-Fi: Skopje offers free public Wi-Fi in certain areas, such as parks, squares, and some cafes and restaurants. Look for signage indicating the availability of public Wi-Fi, and you may need to register or provide some basic information to access the network.

Mobile Data: If you prefer constant internet access while exploring Skopje, consider purchasing a local SIM card with a data plan. Several mobile network providers offer prepaid SIM cards that can be used in unlocked devices. Visit one of the provider's stores or authorized resellers to purchase a SIM card and select a data plan that suits your needs.

Internet Cafes: While internet cafes are not as common as they used to be, you can still find a few in Skopje. These establishments provide computers with internet access for a fee, allowing you to browse, check emails, or complete any online tasks.

Please note that the availability and quality of Wi-Fi may vary depending on the location. It's always a good idea to have a backup plan, such as a local SIM card, to ensure a reliable internet connection when needed.

15.5 Emergency Services and Medical Assistance

When visiting Skopje, it's important to be aware of the emergency services and medical assistance available to ensure your safety and well-being. Here's what you need to know:

Emergency Numbers: In case of an emergency, dial 112, the universal emergency number, which connects you to police, fire, and medical services. English is widely understood by emergency operators.

Medical Facilities: Skopje has several hospitals and medical centers that provide a range of medical services. The public healthcare system is complemented by private clinics and specialized medical facilities. If you require medical assistance, it's advisable to contact your travel insurance provider or the local embassy for guidance on recommended medical facilities.

Pharmacies: Pharmacies, known as "Apoteka" in Macedonian, can be found throughout Skopje. They stock a wide range of over-the-counter medications and basic medical supplies. Some pharmacies may have a 24-hour service, while others have regular operating hours.

Travel Insurance: It's highly recommended to have comprehensive travel insurance that covers medical expenses, including emergency evacuation if needed. Before traveling, ensure that your insurance policy covers your intended activities and any pre-existing medical conditions.

Language Barrier: English is spoken and understood by many people in Skopje, especially in tourist areas. However, it's advisable to carry a phrasebook or language translation app to communicate basic needs in case of emergencies.

It's always wise to prioritize your safety and well-being when traveling. Familiarize yourself with emergency services, know the location of medical facilities, and ensure you have appropriate travel insurance coverage to provide peace of mind during your visit to Skopje.

15.6 Local Customs and Etiquette

Understanding the local customs and etiquette when visiting Skopje can help you navigate social interactions and show respect for the local culture. Here are some key points to keep in mind:

Greetings: When meeting someone for the first time, a handshake is a common form of greeting. It's customary to address people using their formal titles and last names unless they indicate otherwise.

Respect for Elders: In Macedonian culture, showing respect for elders is highly valued. It's customary to offer your seat to an older person on public transportation and show deference to their opinions and experiences.

Dress Code: Skopje is a relatively conservative city, and it's advisable to dress modestly, especially when visiting religious sites or government buildings. Avoid wearing revealing or provocative clothing, and opt for more conservative attire.

Table Manners: When dining in Skopje, it's considered polite to wait for the host to invite you to sit and start eating. Keep your hands visible on the table, and avoid resting your elbows on it. It's customary to finish your plate as a sign of appreciation for the meal.

Respecting Religious Sites: Skopje is home to several religious sites, including mosques, churches, and monasteries. When visiting these places, dress modestly and remove your shoes if required. Respect any rules or guidelines provided by the religious institution.

Photography Etiquette: When taking photos in Skopje, be respectful of people's privacy and ask for permission before taking close-up shots of individuals. Some religious sites may prohibit photography inside, so always check for any signage or ask for permission.

Language: Macedonian is the official language in Skopje. While many people in tourist areas speak English, it's always appreciated to learn a few basic phrases in Macedonian, such as greetings and thank you.Consider learning basic Albanian phrases to accommodate the city's large Albanian minority as well.

By respecting the local customs and etiquette, you can foster positive interactions and create memorable experiences during your visit to Skopje.

15.7 North or Not?

The Macedonian naming issue has been a long-standing topic of debate and political contention. It primarily revolves around the use of the name "Macedonia" and its implications for the identity and territorial claims of the region. The dispute originated from concerns raised by Greece, which has a region in its northern territory also called Macedonia. Greece argued that the use of the name "Macedonia" by its neighboring country could imply territorial claims over its own region of Macedonia and the cultural heritage associated with it.

To resolve this dispute, an agreement was reached between the two countries in 2018, known as the Prespa Agreement. According to the agreement, the country formerly known as the Republic of Macedonia would be renamed as the Republic of North Macedonia. This change was made to address Greece's concerns and establish a distinction between the two regions.

When dealing with official documents, international organizations, or formal contexts, the name Republic of North Macedonia is used to adhere to the terms of the Prespa Agreement and avoid any diplomatic complications.

However, it's important to note that within the country itself, Macedonians still refer to their homeland as Macedonia in casual conversation. They have a strong cultural and historical connection to the name, which predates the naming dispute. Therefore, when visiting Macedonia, it is common for locals to refer to their country as Macedonia and not North Macedonia.

As a visitor, it's important to be aware of the naming issue and the sensitivities surrounding it. When engaging in conversations with locals, it is advisable to refer to the country as Macedonia, as that is how it is commonly understood and used in everyday language. This demonstrates respect for the local culture and acknowledges the significance of the name in the Macedonian identity.

By understanding and respecting the naming issue, visitors can foster positive interactions and connections with the people of Macedonia while appreciating the rich cultural heritage and history of the region.

15.8 Safety and Security

Skopje is generally a safe city to visit, but it's important to take common-sense precautions to ensure your safety and security. Here are some tips to keep in mind:

Personal Belongings: Keep your belongings secure and be mindful of your surroundings, particularly in crowded areas and public transportation. Avoid displaying valuable items or carrying large amounts of cash.

Transportation: Use licensed taxis or reputable ride-sharing services when traveling around Skopje. Always confirm the fare before starting the journey. If using public transportation, be vigilant of your belongings and be aware of pickpocketing risks.

Emergency Services: Save the local emergency numbers in your phone, including 112 for general emergencies, 192 for police, and 193 for fire and rescue. Familiarize yourself with the location of the nearest police station and hospital.

Scams: Like in any tourist destination, be cautious of common scams targeting travelers. Be wary of strangers offering unsolicited assistance or deals that seem too good to be true. Use trusted sources for booking accommodations, tours, and activities.

Nighttime Safety: Exercise caution when out at night, especially in unfamiliar areas. Stick to well-lit and populated areas, and avoid walking alone in isolated or poorly lit areas.

Local Laws: Familiarize yourself with the local laws and regulations of Skopje. Respect the cultural and religious customs, and adhere to any rules in public places or religious sites.

Travel Insurance: It's strongly recommended to have comprehensive travel insurance that covers medical expenses, trip cancellation or interruption, and personal belongings. Check the coverage details and ensure it meets your needs before your trip.

By staying alert, using common sense, and taking necessary precautions, you can have a safe and enjoyable experience exploring the beautiful city of Skopje.

Wrapping Up

Thank you for joining us on this virtual journey through Skopje, the vibrant capital of North Macedonia. We hope that this travel guide has provided you with valuable insights and inspiration to explore this captivating city.

Skopje is a place where history intertwines with modernity, where the echoes of the past can be heard amidst the bustling streets and striking architecture. From the majestic stone bridge that spans the Vardar River to the imposing fortress that stands guard over the city, Skopje is a living testament to its rich and diverse heritage.

As you wander through the Old Bazaar, let the scent of spices and the vibrant colors of the market stalls transport you to another time. Immerse yourself in the cultural tapestry that weaves together Macedonian, Ottoman, and Balkan influences, as you sample delicious traditional cuisine and engage in lively conversations with friendly locals.

Skopje is also a city that embraces the future with open arms. Marvel at the awe-inspiring Skopje 2014 project, where grand statues and neoclassical buildings redefine the city's skyline, creating a unique blend of the old and the new. Discover the lively nightlife scene, where music fills the air and the energy of the city comes alive.

Beyond the city limits, Skopje offers breathtaking natural landscapes that are waiting to be explored. Venture into the nearby Matka Canyon and be captivated by its tranquil waters, towering cliffs, and hidden caves. Explore the scenic mountain ranges that surround the city, where hiking trails and outdoor adventures await.

Whether you're a history enthusiast, a nature lover, or simply a curious traveler, Skopje has something to offer everyone. Its charm lies in its ability to surprise and inspire, inviting you to peel back its layers and uncover the hidden gems that make it truly unique.

As your Skopje adventure comes to a close, we hope that the memories you've made and the experiences you've had will stay with you long after you've left. We encourage you to continue exploring, to seek out new destinations, and to embrace the joy of discovering the world.
Safe travels, and until we meet again on another exciting journey!

Printed in Great Britain
by Amazon

30577374R00095